A POCKET GUIDE

A POCKET GUIDE

ROMAN WALES

WILLIAM MANNING

CARDIFF
UNIVERSITY OF WALES PRESS
THE WESTERN MAIL
2001

Published by the University of Wales Press and The Western Mail.

British Library Cataloguing in Publication Data
A catalogue record for this book is available from the British Library

ISBN 0-7083-1675-1

Front cover: Ivory tragic mask from Caerleon (by permission of the National Museums & Galleries of Wales). Aerial photograph of the amphitheatre at Caerleon (by permission of Skyscan)

Cover design by Chris Neale
Typeset by the University of Wales Press
Printed in Great Britain by Cambrian Printers, Aberystwyth

Contents

Acknowledgements

It is a pleasure to acknowledge the help which I have received from the staff of the University of Wales Press – Duncan Campbell, Susan Jenkins, Ceinwen Jones and Liz Powell. I am greatly indebted to my colleague Howard Mason for drawing the maps used in this book and for permission to reproduce his reconstructions of Caerleon and the Whitton villa. I am also most grateful to Richard Brewer, Evan Chapman and Edward Besley of the National Museum of Wales for their help in assembling the illustrations.

The author and publishers wish to thank the following copyright holders who have kindly permitted the reproduction of their photographs and drawings:

The Archaeology and Art Committee of the Board of Celtic Studies of the University of Wales and the University of Wales Press: reconstructions of the gate and granaries at Usk (Martin Dugdale), from William H. Manning, *Report on the Excavations at Usk 1965–1976: The Fortress Excavations 1968–1971* (Cardiff: University of Wales Press, 1981); plans and reconstructions of the Iron Age and Roman phases of the Whitton villa (Howard Mason), from Michael G. Jarrett and Stuart Wrathmell, *Whitton: An Iron Age and Roman Farmstead in South Glamorgan* (Cardiff: University of Wales Press, 1981); plans of four Roman forts (Maureen Manning), from V. E. Nash-Williams, *The Roman Frontier in Wales*, 2nd edition, M. G. Jarrett (ed.) (Cardiff: University of Wales Press, 1969).

The National Museum of Wales: plan of Caerleon; photographs of the Paulinus Stone; altar to Mars Ocelus; Trajanic inscription from Caerleon; coin of Magnus Maximus; the Llyn Cerrig Bach gang chain; the intaglio from Caerleon; the Caerleon Victory; the view of the excavations at Caerwent; the Roman legionary (Ermine Street Guard); the Roman auxiliary (Ermine Street Guard); the tragic mask from Caerleon.

School of History and Archaeology, Cardiff University, and Viscount Bledisloe: photograph of the Lydney dog.

Cadw: Welsh Historic Monuments: Crown Copyright: plan of Caerwent; photograph of the walls of Caerwent.

Skyscan Balloon Photography: aerial photograph of the Caerleon Amphitheatre.

To

Christopher

who grew up with Roman Wales

Preface

In writing this book my aim was to provide an introduction to the history and archaeology of Roman Wales which would interest both general readers and students. As it is not possible to cover all aspects of the subject in a book of this length, I have concentrated on those things which seem to me to characterize Roman Wales, and to give enough background information to enable the reader to understand how a Roman province functioned, and, in particular, how Wales related to the rest of *Britannia*. Wherever possible I have avoided using Latin and other technical terms, but this is not always possible and when I have used them their meaning is explained where they first appear.

I have used the old pre-1974 counties of Wales to explain geographical positions of the sites referred to in this book, save for the few cases where their replacements have very similar boundaries.

Anyone writing a work such as this is indebted to too many people, living and dead, to be able to thank them all by name, although no one is more conscious of the debt I owe them than I am. I must, however, thank my wife, who read much of the text to its great benefit, and, in particular, Dr Peter Webster who, despite many other commitments, found the time to read the typescript and whose suggestions and corrections have been of the greatest help to me.

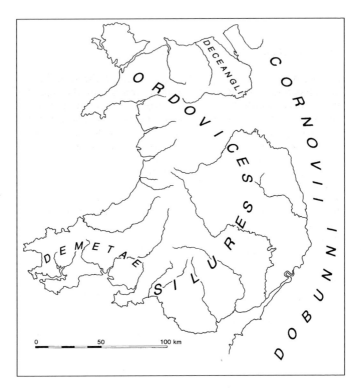

The tribes of Wales and the Marches at the time of the Roman conquest.

1 Prelude: Iron Age Wales

The background to Roman Wales

Wales did not exist as a political unit either in the Iron Age or Roman period; to the Romans it was the area occupied by a group of four tribes which their army first reached in about AD 47 after four years of campaigning. What they found was both similar to, and slightly different from, what they had already encountered in central and southern England. A century of contact with the Roman world had profoundly influenced the tribes of south-eastern England, while scarcely touching those in the west. The Roman Empire offered a wide range of material goods which the Britons found highly attractive; manufactured products such as those listed by the Greek geographer Strabo, 'ivory bracelets and necklaces, amber and glassware and similar pretty trifles'. Surprisingly he omits wine which the Britons appear to have valued above all else. The possession of such luxuries became a status symbol for the native aristocracies who paid for them by exporting raw materials, conveniently listed by Strabo: corn, cattle, gold, silver and iron, hides, slaves and hunting dogs. At the same time some of the tribal rulers formed political alliances with Rome – alliances which were probably very useful to the Romans when, after a century of vacillation, they launched their invasion in AD 43. But the tribes of Wales lay too far to the west to have had direct contact with the Romans before the conquest, and if they saw any of the desirable things which originated in the Roman world it was as gifts from their eastern neighbours, or as payment for the raw materials such as the metals mentioned by Strabo, or prisoners captured in the frequent wars with other tribes who could be sold on to the Romans as slaves.

Our knowledge of the late Iron Age in Wales is almost entirely dependent on archaeology. Such references as there are in Classical writings were written after the conquest and they offer little detailed information on the natives or their customs. At the time of the Roman conquest Wales was divided among four main tribes. In the south-east were the Silures with the Demetae to the west of them. Central and north-west Wales was occupied by the Ordovices whose territory extended into Shropshire and

1

The Silures

The only description of the early inhabitants of Wales given by an ancient writer is that of the Silures in Tacitus' *Agricola*: 'the swarthy faces of the Silures, the tendency of their hair to curl and the fact that Spain lies opposite, all lead one to believe that Spaniards crossed in ancient times and occupied the land.' The suggested link with Spain is the result of the mistaken Roman belief that south-western Britain faced Spain, but the description is likely to be accurate enough as it probably came from Agricola, Tacitus' father-in-law, who had known the Silures at first hand when he governed Britain.

Herefordshire. These tribes survived into the Roman period, but the fourth, the Deceangli of Flintshire, is mentioned only during the conquest phase and the Romans probably added their territory to that of the Cornovii, who occupied the northern marches of Wales, when they organized the local administration of the province at the end of the first century.

Hillforts and other settlements

The most obvious physical remains of the Iron Age in Wales are the hillforts. The term is a loose one and means no more than an Iron Age site which was defended by ramparts of earth or stone, usually with an external ditch. Such sites vary greatly in their size and the strength of their defences. In the east of England hillforts had largely passed out of use by the time of the Roman invasion, but as the Roman army moved further west it found that hillforts were still favoured in the west of England and Wales.

A glance at a map of Iron Age Wales reveals that hillforts are not evenly distributed throughout the country. The greatest concentration is in the Marches where a chain of forts runs south from Prestatyn along the eastern edge of the Welsh hills to the Severn estuary. A second, but more diffuse group, follows the coastal lowlands of south Wales as far as Pembrokeshire and Cardiganshire. Here there are many small enclosures with relatively slight defences which, although conventionally called hillforts, are manifestly not comparable to the great hillforts of the Marches either in size, strength or, presumably, function. In the north there is a scatter along the coast, with an important group in the Llŷn Peninsula. Inland their distribution is more limited and appears to have been controlled by the availability of land suitable for cultivation; the main group lies around Brecon where there is a relatively large area of good agricultural land. In fact the distribution of most of the Welsh hillforts appears to have been governed by the availability of land suitable for arable farming. Modern agricultural practices over much of central Wales have tended to favour pastoral farming, but records show that before the advent of the railways these areas produced substantial amounts of grain, and there is little doubt that in both the Iron Age and Roman periods mixed farming would have been the norm in most parts of Wales.

If the distribution of hillforts reflects the distribution of people then the high moors of south Wales and the mountains of north Wales had a very low population for they are almost devoid of hillforts. These areas may have been used for summer grazing, but such activity leaves little trace in the archaeological record. The topography of much of Wales, with areas of good farming land in the valleys separated by large expanses of moors and mountains, will have produced a fragmented pattern of settlement which may have made central control more difficult than in less rugged landscapes. The fact that the vast majority of Welsh hillforts are relatively small, often enclosing a hectare (2.5 acres) or less, also suggests that they were used by small groups of people who did not need large enclosures and probably lacked the resources to build them.

In England we know that hillforts were only one form of settlement, and this was also the case in Wales, although we have fewer details than in England. In the north-west there are large numbers of stone-walled huts, usually arranged in groups although individual ones are known. Dating such huts is not easy, but recent excavations have shown that many date from the Iron Age with the settlement often, perhaps normally, continuing to be used in the Roman period. The fact that they are commonly found in the same areas as hillforts but at lower levels indicates that they complemented the population patterns suggested by the hillforts rather than extended them into different areas. The situation in the south-west of Wales tends to confirm this diversity, for here we find relatively few true hillforts but large numbers of small, lightly defended enclosures, often called *raths*. Their status in the Iron

3

Age hierarchy is debatable, but they were probably the homes of an Iron Age 'squirearchy', families of some status who were dependent on their own land for their living.

Common sense suggests that there will have been settlements in the valleys of mid-Wales, but these areas were intensively cultivated in later periods and this has destroyed or masked the slight remains of these settlements. The fact that so much of Wales is under rough pasture, which is a poor medium for producing crop marks, means that aerial photography, which has been so successful in discovering Iron Age settlements on the arable lands of England, largely fails us in Wales. Only in the Severn valley has it produced evidence of numbers of small enclosures, and, while most of these remain unexcavated, they suggest that the English pattern extended into eastern Wales. Further south we find small enclosures in the Vale of Glamorgan, the best example being at Whitton Cross Roads, north of Barry, where the excavation of a Roman villa revealed that the site had begun as a small late Iron Age farmstead enclosed by a bank and ditch (Chapter 9).

Relatively few Welsh hillforts have been extensively excavated, but, where they have, the internal arrangements appear to have been similar to those found in England with two basic types of building, round houses and small rectangular granaries supported on four thick corner posts. The majority of the huts were built of wood, but in a few forts, such at Tre'r Ceiri in the Llŷn Peninsula, stone was used for the walls. The shrines known from a few English hillforts, such as Danebury, Hampshire, have not been found in Welsh hillforts, but this probably reflects the limited scale of excavations in Wales rather than a genuine absence.

Iron Age society

Any discussion of the social structure of the Iron Age is bound to be largely speculative, but it is possible to reach a number of fairly firm conclusions. Whenever a Roman writer refers to the political system of a tribe in Britain it was monarchical, which suggests that this was the normal arrangement. Rulers, who could be kings or queens, were chosen from the families of their predecessors. Their power largely rested on their ability to retain the loyalty of the tribal aristocracy and their followers, and to do this gifts and feasting were probably as necessary as statesmanship and military prowess. As Julius Caesar noted of the Gallic nobility: 'The greater their rank and resources the more dependants and clients do they possess. This is the only source of their influence and power.' The sheer number of hillforts in Wales suggests that warfare was common, although it probably took the form of raiding for loot, cattle and women rather than major campaigns of conquest. The economy of almost all Iron Age settlements was based on agriculture, in most cases a mixture of stock (cattle, sheep and pigs) and cereal cultivation, the proportion probably varying with the nature of the land. The situation was neatly encapsulated by the Greek writer Polybius writing of the Gauls: 'They were exclusively occupied with war and agriculture.'

The literary evidence suggests that there was a system of alliances between the tribes, with the smaller ones owing an obligation of duty to a larger one. However, the ancient writers make it clear that loyalty in this client/patron system always depended on the ability of the patron to supply the client with desirable things, whether this was loot, food or reflected glory. It was probably the necessity of maintaining military prestige, and the loot which resulted from successful raids on other tribes, which made warfare endemic in the Iron Age.

Today we probably find Iron Age art the most attractive aspect of their culture. The origins of this art lay in the early La Tène cultures of the fifth century BC in central Europe and eastern Gaul, but it came to permeate Iron Age society in Britain. Although it is seen at its finest on metalwork, it is also found on pottery, and was probably equally common on organic objects. It is composed of curvilinear designs which are used to create a wide variety of elegant patterns. Human or animal forms were generally avoided, but when they do appear they were transformed into part of the overall design, and today we sometimes feel uncertain if they are real or exist only in our imagination. A number of fine pieces are known from Wales, including some from the great late Iron Age votive deposit found at Llyn Cerrig Bach on Anglesey.

There is little doubt that in the Iron Age art was associated with religion, even if the precise nature of the link eludes us. Our knowledge of the religion of this period is based partly on the accounts of Classical authors and partly on the evidence of archaeology. Unfortunately, the former were biased by being written by outsiders who regarded Iron Age peoples as barbarians. When we are dealing with Britain we are still further handicapped by the fact that almost all the surviving literature refers to the Gauls or Germans, and we must be cautious in assuming that

5

what was recorded of those peoples necessarily applies to Wales. However, by combining all our sources and trying to steer a course between excessive gullibility and undue scepticism we may hope to build up a reasonably accurate picture of Iron Age religion, albeit a picture which is stronger on ritual than theology!

In the main it was a simple religion, lacking the philosophical concepts found in Eastern religions. Some of the gods seem to have been worshipped throughout much of Iron Age Europe, while others were extremely localized, spirits of a particular area, or of a spring or a lake. Many of the elements found in other primitive religions were present: the need to renew the fertility of animals and crops, and to propitiate gods who were often hostile and who had to be placated by the sacrifice of animals and treasure. The ancient authors are united in asserting that human sacrifice played an important part in this religion, and the evidence of archaeology supports them. Sacrifice is the only reasonable explanation for the well-known bog burials and the skeletons of people who had been deliberately buried beneath the ramparts of hillforts. Such burials are made even more striking by the fact that the Iron Age is a period in which normal burials are rarely found. Magic, the taking of omens and the absolute observance of ritual were of prime importance, and ensuring that the correct procedures were followed was the responsibility of that most misunderstood of all Iron Age groups, the Druids. All that we know of them is derived from Classical writers, especially Caesar, and the picture which those writers give is both confused and confusing. The Druids appear to have controlled the rituals on which Iron Age religion depended, including human sacrifice. Their culture lacked written records, and their training, with its emphasis on memorizing detail, gave them a key position in that society. One significant fact which Caesar provides is that many of them came to Britain for their training, and, as we shall see, it is possible that Anglesey was of particular importance in this respect.

Classical writers refer to sacrifices in sacred woods and pools in Gaul and archaeological discoveries suggest that the custom of depositing offerings in water was common in Britain. Wales provides one of the most spectacular examples of this custom in the great collection of bronze and ironwork found in a pool at Llyn Cerrig Bach, Anglesey.

The Llyn Cerrig Bach deposit

This great assemblage of bronze and iron objects, most of which probably date from between the second century BC and the first century AD, was dredged from a small lake in 1942 during the construction of the RAF airfield at Valley on Anglesey. It includes a large amount of bronze and iron horse-gear and elaborate vehicle fittings, as well as swords, spearheads, a shield boss, a group of iron bars of the type known as 'currency bars' (which may or may not have been their function) and an iron sickle. However, the most spectacular piece is the gang chain, some 3 metres (10 feet) long with five neck-rings. It may have been connected with the Roman world's insatiable demand for slaves, which made slave raiding a profitable occupation among the Iron Age tribes of Britain in the years before the Roman conquest.

There is no doubt that the whole group was the result of one or, more probably, a series of religious ceremonies during which the metalwork was thrown from a rocky ledge into the lake. It is probably the clearest example in Britain of a votive deposit resulting from the Iron Age veneration for water. Radiocarbon dating has recently dated some animal bones found with the metalwork to the third century BC, and this suggests that the rite also involved animal sacrifice. The value of the material thrown into Llyn Cerrig Bach must have been very high, a fact which suggests that the site was of more than merely local importance.

2 The Arrival of the Romans

The invasion of Britain

The Roman invasion of Britain took place in AD 43. The core of the invading army consisted of four legions (Second Augusta, Ninth Hispana, Fourteenth Gemina and Twentieth Valeria) each of about 5,500 men. These provided the heavy infantry and they were complemented by an equal number of auxiliary troops, who formed the light infantry and cavalry. A Roman army of the mid-first century AD was a formidable military force and the Britons were no match for it in the open field. Within weeks of their landing at Richborough in Kent, the Romans had inflicted a major defeat on the British army commanded by the leaders of the tribes of south-eastern England, Caratacus and Togodumnus. Their next target was the enemy's capital at Camulodunum and the successful assault on it was directed by Claudius himself, a fact which may or may not have helped the Roman commanders. By that time Togodumnus was dead, but Caratacus survived to remain a thorn in the Roman side for some years to come.

After the fall of Camulodunum Claudius returned to Rome, and the army commander and first governor of the new province of Britannia, Aulus Plautius, was left to bring the rest of the country under Roman control. Some tribes welcomed the invaders and their rulers were granted the status of Roman clients, among them Cartimandua, queen of the Brigantes of northern England, and Prasutagus, king of the Iceni of East Anglia. But not all tribes favoured the Romans and these had to be subdued by force. Three army columns, each centred on a legion, struck out to the north-east, to the north-west and to the south-west; the fourth legion, the Twentieth Valeria, remaining in garrison at Colchester, the capital of the new province.

The conquest of Wales begins

By AD 47 most of southern and central England was under Roman control. The north was held for them by Cartimandua, but to the west the tribes of Wales remained outside the province. In that year Aulus Plautius' term of office came to an end and he was replaced by Ostorius Scapula, an experienced general and a competent administrator. We do not know if he planned an immediate attack on Wales, but in the event the enemy took the initiative, and Scapula arrived in Britain to find that an allied tribe had been attacked. Unfortunately our source, the historian Tacitus, tells us neither the name of the attacker nor that of the attacked, although the fact that Scapula's first act was to bring the area between the Rivers Trent and Severn under Roman control suggests that the trouble was in the west Midlands, and this is confirmed by his next move, an attack on the Deceangli of Flintshire. Whether they had acted on their own, or, as seems more likely, in concert with their more powerful neighbours, the Ordovices, we do not know. Perhaps we are wrong in seeking to see a conspiracy against the Romans behind this attack, for the Deceangli may have done no more than what they had been doing for generations, raiding a richer neighbour in search of loot. If so they soon learned that the rules of the game had been changed.

Dealing with the Deceangli does not seem to have caused Scapula many problems, but this was not to prove the case with the Ordovices and their southern neighbours the Silures, on whom he now turned. For reasons which are not recorded in the surviving sections of Tacitus, the armies of both tribes were under the overall command of Caratacus, the king who had been defeated by the Romans four years before. Tacitus never refers to kings of the Silures or the Ordovices, but this is probably the result of his literary technique rather than an indication that they had no kings of their own. By concentrating on a heroic figure, who appears at various points in his story, Tacitus avoided confusing his readers with too many barbaric names, while creating a personification of native resistance, a noble savage whose misfortunes could be, and were, used to heighten the overall effect.

The description which Tacitus gives us of these campaigns, which continued over several years, is dramatic but generalized. Ostorius' first objective was the suppression of the Silures, and to accomplish this he brought the Twentieth Legion, previously at Camulodunum, up to the front, building a new headquarters for it at Kingsholm, near Gloucester. At this stage in the conquest the legions did not build the great fortresses seen in later periods, but were divided among a number of smaller, vexillation fortresses, each of about 6 hectares (15 acres). Camulodunum, the only known exception to this rule, was the provincial capital and

The historian Tacitus

Cornelius Tacitus (AD 56/7–after 112) was the greatest Roman historian of the early Empire and a senator who rose to the highest office as governor of the Province of Asia. In 77 he married the daughter of Agricola, who was about to become governor of Britain, and his eulogistic biography of his father-in law published in AD 98 was one of his earliest works, and is almost our only source of information on Britain between *c*.70 and 90. His greatest work was a history of Rome in the first century AD. Unfortunately large parts are now lost and what remains is divided into two works, *The Annals* covering AD 14–69, and the *Histories* dealing with the years 69–96, although only the section for 69–71 survives. Tacitus is a brilliant and idiosyncratic literary stylist, who, like all ancient historians, uses devices which are alien to our ideas of how history should be written. In particular he has no hesitation in putting fictional speeches into the mouths of historical characters. In his accounts of Britain he strongly favoured governors who were active in the field, which tends to bias his account of the conquest.

Ancient historians were trying to write works of literature which would hold the interest of their original readers and not bore them with tedious descriptions of native tribes and detailed topography, and in reading Tacitus one must always remember that he was a Roman historian writing for Roman readers.

required special treatment. Since legionary headquarters were usually placed some way behind the front line, we may assume that at this stage the main action was taking place in the Welsh Marches, probably to the north of the Forest of Dean. Excavations on the hillfort at Bredon Hill, near Evesham, revealed evidence of a massacre in the gateway where Roman weapons were found, suggesting that this was one of the hillforts which the Roman army took in these campaigns.

At some point in this war, which lasted until AD 51, Caratacus moved north into Ordovician territory, probably the Marches of mid-Wales. Here he staked everything on one great battle which he lost. Tacitus' description of the action is dramatic but lacking in detail. The Britons took up position on a hill with mountains behind and a river in front, a description which fits too many hills in Wales for this one to be identified. At the end of the battle Caratacus' wife, daughter and brothers were Roman prisoners, but he had escaped to seek refuge with Cartimandua, queen of the Brigantes. In so doing he committed a major error of judgement, for Cartimandua was a Roman ally and she chose, wisely as history was to show, to hand Caratacus over to them and so ensure their future loyalty to her.

The new military system

The defeat of Caratacus did not bring about the immediate subjugation of either the Ordovices or the Silures, and we read of ambushes of auxiliary units developing into full-scale battles which were only ended when the Romans brought their legionaries into action. In the midst of these campaigns, in the year 52, Ostorius Scapula died, in Tacitus' words 'worn out by anxiety'. His successor, Didius Gallus, arrived to find that the position had deteriorated since his predecessor's death, for the Silures had defeated a legion, an achievement of which they were justly proud, although in the event Gallus was able to restore control without much difficulty. Tacitus is our only source for the governorship of Gallus and he damns him with faint praise, probably because he spent most of his time reorganizing the military arrangements in the province which Scapula had left in disarray. Roman governors had great independence in routine matters, but the framework within which they worked was decided in Rome. If Gallus did not attempt new conquests it was because his orders excluded such action, a restriction which may have resulted from Claudius' death in 54 and the minority of his successor Nero.

Until recently we were in the unusual position of having literary accounts of these wars but little archaeological evidence to complement them. Then in 1965 the remains of a legionary fortress was found at Usk, to be followed over the next thirty years by the discovery of a series of new forts. Most are thought to have been built in a programme of fort construction undertaken by Gallus on the borders of Wales, although some probably post-date him and a few may be slightly earlier. The military forces on the Welsh front were centred on two legions, Fourteenth Gemina in the northern Marches and Twentieth Valeria in the south, and these

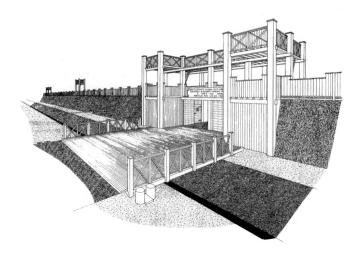

Reconstruction of the exterior of the timber east gate of the legionary fortress at Usk in c.AD 60. (Drawn by Martin Dugdale)

were supported by an equal number of auxiliaries – a substantial army if it could be concentrated in one place, but less formidable when units were detached to garrison the newly conquered territory. During Scapula's campaigns the legions were probably divided among a number of vexillation fortresses, possibly brigaded with auxiliaries to create small armies capable of responding to local problems. Kingsholm, now part of Gloucester, was the key one in the south, although others may yet be found further west, for example at Weston-under-Penyard (Ariconium), or Kenchester (Magnis), both sites in Herefordshire where early Roman material has been found. In the north, vexillation fortresses are known at Wall in Staffordshire, Kinvaston near Penkridge in Staffordshire and Leighton, Shropshire, all to the east of Wroxeter on Watling Street, the main military route into north Wales. We know less about the smaller forts which housed the bulk of the auxiliaries. Several have been found to the east of the River Severn in the west Midlands, but there are fewer to the west and we do not know if they were built by Scapula or Gallus.

The forts of south Wales

Once Gallus had restored the military situation he initiated a major rearrangement of the Roman forces on the Welsh frontier. In this he had two objectives, to stop the Silures and Ordovices raiding the Roman province, and to create the bases which would be needed if Nero ordered new campaigns in Wales. His solution was simple, but effective: the creation of a series of auxiliary forts blocking the major valleys leading into the hills of east Wales. Such forts would prevent the tribesmen from raiding the peoples already under Roman control while creating the springboards necessary for the Roman army to be able to harass the enemy or launch new campaigns. These forts formed the front line, but they were supported by two great legionary fortresses each large enough to hold an entire legion. Their construction must have meant the closure of many, although perhaps not all, of the existing vexillation fortresses. In the north a fortress was built on the Welsh border at Wroxeter, Shropshire, to give the Romans control of the Severn valley, one of the main routes into north Wales from the Midlands.

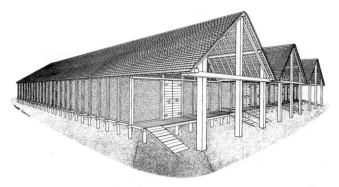

Reconstruction of three timber granaries in the legionary fortress at Usk in c. AD 60. (Drawn by Martin Dugdale)

In the south the Twentieth Valeria was moved forward to Usk, the point at which the main road from England, which then ran to the north of the Forest of Dean, entered the Usk valley. It was a site which controlled the routes south to the coastal lowlands and north to Abergavenny and the hills of Breconshire. The road to

13

Usk from Gloucester, where it crossed the River Severn, was secured by forts at Monmouth, and possibly at Weston-under-Penyard. Another fort at Abergavenny blocked the valley where the River Usk passes between the Black Mountains and the Brecon Beacons. The Golden Valley, which cuts through the eastern end of the Black Mountains, was controlled by forts at Kentchurch and Abbey Dore, although these are too close together to be contemporary. These early forts were built of timber with earthen ramparts and they could be replaced with relative ease if the strategic situation altered.

The only fort known on the coastal plain of south Wales at this time was at Cardiff, where a large fort was built on the site later occupied by Cardiff Castle. By placing a fort there the Romans were able to control movement through the coastal lowlands as well as along the Taff valley which leads into the hills of east Glamorgan. The fort's unusually large size suggests that it probably held a mixed garrison of auxiliaries or auxiliaries brigaded with legionaries. It probably also served as a harbour for a fleet operating in the Severn estuary. It must have been at about this time that the Romans occupied the Iron Age coastal fort at Sudbrook near Caldicot, presumably to ensure a secure landing point for a ferry crossing from England. The Romans regularly used fleets to support their land forces, and their occupation of Sudbrook and a number of sites on the English side of the estuary suggests that they moved a fleet into the west early in their campaigns.

In the event of trouble it would have been possible for these auxiliary forts to have been supported by the legion at Usk, but this would not have been so easy further north in the Wye valley. A legion could normally march about twenty miles in a day, and while this could be increased in an emergency, the topography of south Wales meant that the route from Usk to the middle Wye valley was inconveniently long if reinforcements were needed in a hurry. This is probably the reason why we find two large forts of around 7 hectares (17 acres) near Hay-on-Wye, where the river flows from the hills of mid-Wales into the more gentle landscape of the borders. Here again the forts are too close to be contemporary, and it is likely that the fort at Clifford was the earlier and that it was replaced by the one at Clyro, which is a better site and not liable to flooding. Slightly further north a fort at Walton, near Presteigne, blocked a minor route into the hills.

14

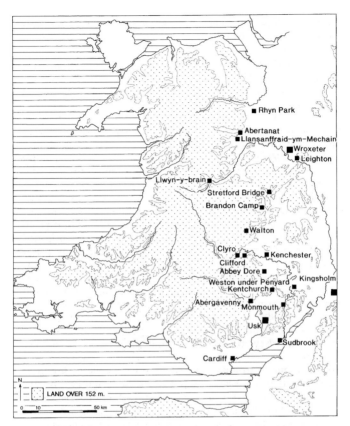

Roman forts in Wales and the Marches before AD 75.

The forts of north Wales

We know less of the forts in the middle and northern Marches which were controlled from the new fortress of the Fourteenth Legion at Wroxeter in the Severn valley. Such evidence as we have suggests that the system was very similar to that in the south. The Severn valley was the key to the north of Wales and the depth of Roman penetration along the valley is shown by the large fort at

Llwyn-y-brain near Caersŵs which must date to this period. Strategically it corresponds to Clyro in the Wye valley, and together they indicate the importance which the Roman army placed on these major river valleys.

The southern limit of the area controlled by the Fourteenth Legion probably lay between the fort at Walton and a small Iron Age hillfort, Brandon Camp in Herefordshire, which the Roman army converted into a fort of their own while leaving the original defences largely untouched. Recent discoveries have shown that the Romans occasionally used Iron Age forts in this way, but such sites are difficult to identify and are usually only found by chance. Brandon Camp is just south of Leintwardine, an area which was of strategic importance as it controlled the Teme valley leading into mid-Wales. Slightly further north a fort at Stretford Bridge blocked another route into mid-Wales.

To the north of Wroxeter, forts at Llansanffraid-ym-Mechain and Abertanat, south of Oswestry, show the importance of the valleys leading into the mountains to the west. These provide another example of forts which are too close together to be con-temporary, and here again we see the Roman willingness to move garrisons quite short distances if they judged it advantageous. The major site to the north of Wroxeter was probably at Rhyn Park, near Chirk, where a vexillation fortress was built just south of the point at which the road to Snowdonia follows the valley of the River Dee into the hills.

Other forts certainly exist in the northern Marches, and it is unlikely that the area around Chester, possibly even Chester itself, was completely neglected. But the framework of the military system is now clear – a chain of forts in the Marches which gave the Roman army almost complete control of all large-scale movement in and out of Wales. Gallus had set the stage for the next act in the conquest of Wales.

3 Victories and Disasters

The conquest resumed

Whatever doubts Nero and his advisers may have had on the wisdom of continuing the conquest of Britain, they had been resolved by AD 57 when Didius Gallus left Britain. He was replaced by Quintus Veranius, an experienced general, who immediately began a major campaign against the Silures, only to die within the year. The fact that he was able to begin a war as soon as he arrived suggests that the preparations had been made by his predecessor. Tacitus condemns the unfortunate Veranius, who had claimed in his will that he would have brought the whole province under Roman control had he lived another two years, a claim which Tacitus clearly regarded as misplaced vanity. A small fort at Dolau (Nantmel) near Llandrindod Wells may well have been built in this, or a later, unrecorded campaign, for it is too close to the late first-century fort at Castell Collen to be of the same date.

Tacitus admired Suetonius Paulinus, Veranius' successor, as a man of action. When Tacitus' narrative begins we find Paulinus and his army already on the shore facing Anglesey, which was, in Tacitus' words, 'a native stronghold and a haven for fugitives', and apparently a centre of the Druids and their followers. The Roman authorities, usually remarkably tolerant of native religions, were implacably opposed to the Druids, largely because they could not tolerate the human sacrifices which formed part of their rites. Tacitus does not describe the campaigns which brought Paulinus to the northern shores of Wales, although the Roman army would never have advanced so far through difficult territory with a long and exposed supply route if they had not already gained control of much of north Wales and checked the Ordovices. Nor does Tacitus record the route taken by the army. The arrangement of forts in the northern marches (Chapter 2) suggests that they used the Dee valley, through Llangollen and Betws-y-coed, passing through Snowdonia to reach the Menai Straits near Conwy or Bangor. The alternative route, north from Wroxeter, which must have been their starting-point, towards Chester and then along the north coast of Wales, is possible but less likely. To cross the Straits they constructed a fleet of flat-bottomed landing craft which ferried the infantry across while the cavalry waded or swam alongside their mounts.

The attack on Anglesey

Tacitus gives a dramatic, even melodramatic, account of the attack on Anglesey:

> The enemy lined the shore: a dense host of armed men, interspersed with women clothed in black, like the Furies, with their hair hanging down, and holding torches in their hands. Round these were the Druids, uttering dire curses, and stretching out their hands towards heaven. These strange sights terrified our soldiers. They stood motionless, as if paralysed, offering their bodies to the blows. At last encouraged by the General, and exhorting each other not to quail before a rabble of female fanatics, they advanced their standards, bore down all resistance, and enveloped the enemy in their own flames. Suetonius imposed a garrison upon the conquered, and cut down the groves devoted to their cruel superstitions: for it was part of their religion to spill the blood of captives on their altars, and to enquire of the Gods by means of human entrails.

Although Tacitus does not record the composition of the army which Paulinus used in this campaign, his description of subsequent events makes it clear that the Fourteenth Legion based at Wroxeter formed the core, together with detachments from the Twentieth, the other legion on the Welsh front. Less is known of the auxiliaries, although his description of the cavalry swimming across the Straits suggests that they included some Batavian cavalry from Holland, who were famous for crossing rivers in this way – an ability which often gave the Romans a tactical advantage in such battles. The fort which Tacitus records on Anglesey remains to be found.

The fact that by AD 60 the Romans had largely broken the military power of both the Silures and the Ordovices suggests that Veranius' claim that he could have completed the conquest of the province had he lived two more years was not the idle boast which Tacitus thought it. Tacitus may have taken it to mean the whole of

Britain, a reasonable interpretation when he wrote at the end of the century after the conquest of much of Scotland, but not when Veranius died. At that time the north of England was ruled by Cartimandua, client queen of the Brigantes, and the 'province' probably meant England and Wales south of her kingdom, and, as we have seen, by AD 60 the campaigns of Paulinus had largely completed the conquest of that area. All that remained was to incorporate the conquered territories into the province, or so it seemed.

The Boudiccan revolt

Paulinus was still savouring his victory in north Wales when the news arrived of a major disaster in eastern England. The trouble had begun with the death of Prasutagus, the client king of the Iceni of East Anglia. Client kingship was a treaty relationship between the Roman senate and the ruler in question. In effect it provided a halfway house between independence and complete Roman control, and the ruler's death usually resulted in the kingdom passing into Roman hands. This was the case with the Iceni, but the governor had left the practicalities to the procurator, the chief financial officer of the province, who handled it with a remarkable degree of incompetence. The kingdom was treated not as a loyal ally which was being welcomed into the Roman commonwealth, but as conquered territory to be exploited as the procurator and his friends saw fit. When the Icenian royal family protested, they were treated with appalling brutality, the widow was flogged and her daughters raped. Unfortunately for the Romans the mistreated wife, Boudicca, was a remarkable woman who proved only too capable of organizing her furious subjects into effective action, and a full-scale revolt erupted.

Suetonius Paulinus was in a difficult position. The only troops he could rely on were those with him in north Wales, some 10,000 men, according to Tacitus. The rest of the Roman troops in Britain were widely dispersed and his efforts to get them to join him failed. The inevitable battle took place somewhere in the Midlands and the Roman troops who, if they had lost, faced certain death, showed all the ruthless efficiency which made them the finest army in the ancient world. The defeat of Boudicca and the massacre of her followers ended the threat to the province, but it revealed with chilling clarity that the Romans had grossly overestimated the extent to which some of the English tribes had accepted their rule, and forced a complete re-evaluation of their policy. One consequence was the award of the title *Victrix* (Victorious) to both the Fourteenth and the Twentieth Legions.

Roman losses in this war had been considerable and large numbers of troops were needed to control the tribes which had revolted; even with the 2,000 legionaries and 5,000 auxiliaries sent by Nero to reinforce the British garrison, it was clear that the Romans could not garrison the whole of Wales as well as England. The result was a decision to abandon the conquest of Wales and return to the frontier created by Gallus. The Boudiccan revolt had gained the Welsh tribes another fourteen years of freedom.

After the revolt

The years which followed the Boudiccan crisis were probably not without military activity in Wales, but the literary references are imprecise, often leaving even the part of Britain involved uncertain. Where we have clear details they concern the collapse of the client kingdom relationship with Cartimandua, who had discarded her husband only to be overthrown by him. By the mid-sixties the aftermath of the Boudiccan revolt had died down and it might have been possible to resume the conquest of Wales, but any such plan was ended when Nero, not hitherto notable as a military figure, decided on a major war with the Parthians, the traditional enemy of Rome in the Middle East. Such a war could not be undertaken without extensive preparations, and assembling the necessary army led to troop movements all over the Empire. Inevitably Britain, with its four legions, was seen as a province from which troops could be drawn, and the Fourteenth Legion and its auxiliaries were moved to the Continent. This decision created a major problem in Britain, for the Fourteenth Legion was at Wroxeter, and its departure meant that the northern Marches were left without a garrison, and, what was equally important, it left the western flank of the Brigantes unguarded at a time when their relations with Rome were approaching a crisis. The Ninth Legion was at Lincoln keeping a watchful eye on the eastern side of Brigantia and moving it would simply have transferred the problem from one side of Britain to the other. But there were two other legions in the province, the Twentieth at Usk and the Second Augusta at Exeter. The solution chosen was a strategic compromise: the Twentieth Legion went from Usk to Wroxeter, and the Second to a new fortress at Gloucester, a position which enabled it to keep an eye both on the south-west of England and the Silures. There is some evidence for an auxiliary cavalry unit being stationed in part of the fortress at Usk at about this time, probably to control the lower Usk valley. Under these circumstances major new campaigns in Britain were out of the question.

Ironically, Nero's eastern war, the cause of all these changes, never even began, for in 69 he was overthrown by a series of military rebellions and the Roman world was racked by civil war. Four emperors claimed the throne within a single year before Vespasian emerged as the victor and the conquest of Britain was resumed.

The completion of the conquest

The years since the Boudiccan revolt had seen steady commercial and political development in most parts of the province, especially in southern and central England. In the north, however, Cartimandua had lost her marital war and the Brigantes were openly hostile to Rome, while in the west the Silures and Ordovices had been given time to repair the damage inflicted on them in the fifties. Vespasian was an able general who had served in Britain early in his career and was familiar with the country, and a military solution seemed the obvious one to him. The result was the decision to complete the conquest, not only of England and Wales, but of Scotland as well. In Tacitus' epigrammatic words, 'there came a succession of great generals and splendid armies, and the hopes of our enemies dwindled'. The first of these generals was Petilius Cerealis who arrived in 71 bringing a new legion, the Second Aduitrix, with him.

The war began with an attack on the Brigantes and by 74, when he departed, Cerealis had pushed the frontier as far north as Carlisle. He was succeeded by an exceptionally able man, Julius Frontinus, whose orders were to resume and complete the conquest of the Silures and Ordovices. It is unlikely that the Roman army had left the Welsh tribes entirely at peace in the sixties; they would have been only too willing to punish any transgressions by the natives, and may have felt that pre-emptive punishment was a sound policy. Nor would the commanders have been averse to

21

Marching camps

Marching camps or temporary camps were the encampments built by a Roman army when on campaign. In theory a camp would have been built each night and used only once, but the numbers known suggest that they were actually constructed rather more sparingly. They are defined by a bank and ditch and, since the troops used tents when on campaign, they do not contain the remains of buildings. The fact that they held an army, rather than a specific unit, means that their area reflects the size of the army involved. In Scotland it has been possible to trace the progress of more than one campaign by comparing the sizes of the marching camps, but this has not proved possible in Wales.

Quite large numbers of marching camps survive in Wales, mainly on the higher land of central Wales where they have not been destroyed by agricultural activity. There is a notable concentration in the area around Wroxeter, but they are conspicuously absent in the west and south-east of Wales, although in the latter case this may be the result of destruction by farming and coal-mining. In most cases their dates are not known, although the majority were probably built before AD 75.

giving their troops some experience of real warfare. But we hear of no major campaigns during that period.

The only account of Frontinus' campaigns, which lasted from 74 to 78, is a terse statement in Tacitus' *Agricola*: 'He (Frontinus) subdued by force of arms the strong and war-like Silures, laboriously triumphing not only over a brave enemy but also over a difficult terrain.' Behind those few words lies a series of campaigns which was even more extensive than Tacitus suggested, and a total reorganization of the army in Wales. The results of Frontinus' conquests will be discussed in the next chapter; what remains is the final act in the conquest of Wales, the campaign of Agricola, Tacitus' distinguished father-in-law. Agricola arrived in the high summer of AD 78 to find that a cavalry unit had been attacked by the Ordovices, and the presence of such a unit in Ordovician territory confirms that Frontinus had campaigned against them as well as the Silures. Tacitus gives an elaborate but rhetorical account of Agricola's actions. He harassed the enemy, cutting to pieces the fighting force of the nation, as Tacitus dramatically puts it, before launching an attack on Anglesey. Although the Romans had occupied the island twenty years earlier, the Boudiccan revolt had forced them to relinquish it. Agricola's arrival took the islanders by surprise – surprise which turned to alarm when his cavalry, no doubt Batavians once again, swam across the straits to launch an entirely unexpected invasion. The result was the immediate surrender of the island. Agricola had one great advantage in this attack for he had been a junior officer on the staff of Suetonius Paulinus at the time of the Boudiccan revolt and had probably taken part in Paulinus' Welsh campaigns. Without lessening the credit due to Agricola, the account suggests that he knew that the opposition would be at best half-hearted. The islanders were unlikely to have forgotten the savagery of the previous Roman attack and they probably did not wish to have it repeated, nor can their resistance have been strengthened by the fact that the rest of the tribe had already been conquered. Had Agricola anticipated a strong resistance, then launching an unsupported, indeed unsupportable, attack using only his cavalry would have been little short of suicidal.

But whatever the merits of his action, it brought the wars in Wales to an end, and with it Wales passes from the pages of Roman history. From now on we are mainly reliant on archaeology for our information.

4 Military Control

Although the campaigns of the mid-seventies completed the Roman conquest of Wales it was necessary to keep the area under military control for some considerable time. Only in the Marches, which had been held for almost thirty years, were the natives sufficiently Romanized for the garrisons to be reduced. The Romans usually controlled newly conquered territory by placing auxiliary forts at strategic points with legionary fortresses some way behind the forts. The problem facing the Romans in the late seventies was that they had to garrison not only Wales, but also Brigantia, and, as Agricola's army moved steadily north, much of Scotland as well.

Changes in the military dispositions in Wales

The basic framework was probably created by Julius Frontinus, but work continued for some years after he had left Britain. The legions were the key to the system. When Frontinus arrived, their bases were at Gloucester and Wroxeter; the fortresses at Usk and Exeter still existed but had only caretaker garrisons, and all, as far as Frontinus was concerned, were in the wrong places. Even Usk, which was in the right area, was in the wrong position, for it was liable to flooding and was too far inland to be supplied by sea. The solution was to move the fortress to Caerleon eight miles to the south of Usk, where the road from England to west Wales crossed the River Usk and met the road running along the Usk valley to Breconshire. The new site also met another critical requirement as it could be supplied by sea. The legion moved there was the Second Augusta, previously at Gloucester.

Wroxeter was equally unsuited to the new military situation. When it had been built the prime military requirement had been control of the Severn valley, but that was no longer the case. With the conquest of north Wales and the Pennines it was necessary to have a base from which both these areas could be supervised, and a new site was chosen at Chester at the mouth of the Dee which was accessible by sea. The legion placed there was the Second Aduitrix, which was relatively new to Britain since it had arrived

Sextus Julius Frontinus

Frontinus was the governor who effectively completed the conquest of Wales and his career illustrates the type of man chosen to govern Britain in the first century. He was probably born in the south of Gaul and in his early years he received the normal varied experience of military and civilian posts. In the later sixties he became a senator and progressed to command a legion, apparently one involved in the suppression of the revolt in Germany in 70. By 74 he had been appointed consul, so was formally qualified to govern a major province, in his case Britain where he spent the next four years (74–8). Unlike that of many governors his career did not end with that appointment. The next few years are obscure, but by 86 he had become governor of Asia (part of western Turkey), the most prestigious of all governorships. Ten years later he took charge of the aqueducts and water supply of Rome, an administrative post of great importance, as a failure of the water supply would have created a major crisis in the city. Subsequently he wrote the standard manual on aqueducts, a work which still survives. But even then his honours were not at an end for he was to hold two further consulships, in 98 and 100, on both occasions with the Emperor Trajan as his fellow consul. To hold one consulship with the emperor was a great honour; to hold two was to mark a man as pre-eminent in the Roman state. He lived for three or four years more, dying, full of honours, in 103 or 104.

in the province only in the early seventies. Unlike Usk, however, Wroxeter was not closed immediately but probably continued as the headquarters of the Twentieth Legion, although from the late seventies the bulk of that legion was in the field in Scotland. Wroxeter only became redundant in the early eighties when a new fortress was founded for the Twentieth Legion at Inchtuthil on the River Tay, after which the fortress and its associated territory was handed over to the Cornovii as the site of their new capital, Viroconium Cornoviorum.

In about AD 87 the Second Aduitrix and its auxiliaries were removed from Britain. This left most of north Wales and the

Pennines without garrisons – an impossible situation which was resolved by withdrawing troops from Scotland and moving the Twentieth Legion from Inchtuthil to Chester. And that, whether they knew it or not, was the end of the Roman dream of conquering the whole of Britain.

The legions were the strategic reserve, vital in the event of an emergency but too important to be dispersed among the forts which garrisoned the newly conquered territories. This was the responsibility of the auxiliaries. Unfortunately most of the existing forts were also in places which had been of strategic importance during the conquest phase but which were largely irrelevant to the requirements of AD 75, with the result that most of the forts mentioned in Chapter 2 were closed. There were a few exceptions: Leintwardine retained its strategic importance, as it was, perhaps surprisingly, to do throughout the Roman period, for it lay in an area which had long been under Roman control. In the south, Abergavenny and Cardiff were too important to be relinquished and new forts were built there as well as a small fort in one corner of the former fortress at Usk . Further north the fort at Llwyn-y-brain was replaced by one at Caersŵs.

Forts in south Wales

The military system created in the fifties had sought to control the native population by blocking the natural routes of communication in east Wales. This idea was to be developed in the new arrangement, only this time the valleys were not blocked but patrolled. To do this effectively required not only new forts but the creation of a new road system linking those forts which allowed the army to patrol the area and move reinforcements to the forts in the event of trouble.

It is clear that we have not found all of the forts built in Wales at this time, but the great majority must be known and they show that the areas which the Romans felt needed the closest surveillance were south-east, central and north-west Wales. The south-west, the north-east and most of the borders were not garrisoned in strength and must have been regarded as loyal to Rome. In the south there is a clear lack of interest in the higher land, such as the Brecon Beacons and Black Mountains, the Mynydd Eppynt, and the hills between the Wye and Usk valleys. These were the areas which were almost devoid of hillforts in the Iron Age, and we may

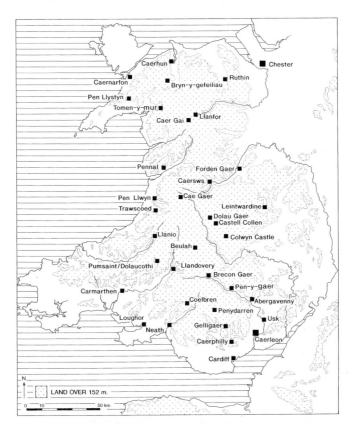

Labels on map:
Caerhun
Chester
Caernarfon
Ruthin
Bryn-y-gefeiliau
Pen Llystyn
Tomen-y-mur
Caer Gai
Llanfor
Pennal
Forden Gaer
Caersws
Pen Llwyn
Cae Gaer
Trawscoed
Leintwardine
Dolau Gaer
Castell Collen
Llanio
Colwyn Castle
Beulah
Pumsaint/Dolaucothi
Llandovery
Brecon Gaer
Pen-y-gaer
Carmarthen
Coelbren
Abergavenny
Penydarren
Loughor
Usk
Neath
Gelligaer
Caerleon
Caerphilly
Cardiff

N
LAND OVER 152 m.
0 10   50 km

Roman forts in Wales and the Marches after AD 75.

assume that they were no more attractive to settlers in the Roman period. Roman forts were intended to control people not barren countryside.

The Usk valley was the key to the system in south Wales, with a chain of forts running north from Caerleon. The first was at Usk, then the next at Abergavenny where the road entered the valley between the Brecon Beacons and the Black Mountains, another lay at Pen-y-gaer where the road emerged into the more open land around Brecon, and the last of the series at Brecon Gaer, west of

27

Brecon, where an unusually large fort was placed at the crossing-point of the main north–south and east–west roads. Further west another line of forts, generally set on the higher land between the river valleys, curves north from Cardiff at Caerphilly, Gelligaer and Penydarren (Merthyr). Penydarren was significant not only because it commanded the upper Taff valley, but because it stood at the southern end of the only practical route through the Brecon Beacons west of Abergavenny. To the west a fort at Neath commanded the main east–west coastal road and probably served as a minor naval base. Further inland there was a fort at Coelbren on the road running from Neath to Brecon Gaer. Taken together these forts effectively controlled the heart of Siluria; no other part of Wales was as strongly garrisoned as this.

A relatively recent discovery is a fort at Loughor to the west of the Gower peninsula, in a position which suggests that it too may have served as a naval base. The only fort known to the west of Loughor is at Carmarthen, but it seems unlikely that the rest of the Demetae were left ungarrisoned and some forts probably remain to be found. However, they are likely to be few in number for, had there been many, some would have been found before now.

The forts at the southern ends of the valleys, Cardiff, Neath, Loughor and Carmarthen, with a possible additional fort at Cowbridge, were linked by a major road which ran through the coastal lowlands from the crossing of the River Wye at Chepstow to the heart of Pembrokeshire. Together they formed a system which controlled the southern edge of Siluria. The fact that Cardiff, Neath, Loughor and Carmarthen were all accessible to sea-going vessels suggests that the Romans needed safe harbours for a fleet operating off the coast of south Wales. We have seen (Chapter 2) that there is evidence for such a fleet in the conquest period, and there is no reason to suppose that it disappeared after 75. Quays have been found on the Usk at Caerleon and they must have been under military control, even if civilians were allowed to use them.

Further north the road continued west from Brecon Gaer to the Tywi valley and a fort at Llandovery on an important road which ran along the valley from Carmarthen to Caersŵs in mid-Wales. From Llandovery the route continued across the hills to another fort at Dolaucothi in the valley of the River Cothi – a site of some importance for it is the only place in Britain where the Romans mined gold (Chapter 11), although whether the fort was put there to guard the mines is an open question. From there the road continued into the valley of the Teifi where it met another road running north along the valley from Carmarthen. A few miles north of this junction, in an area where there is a concentration of hillforts, we find a fort at Llanio.

Forts in mid-Wales

The forts of mid-Wales form less distinct systems, in part because we are ignorant of some of the roads which linked them. From Llandovery a major road ran north-east via a fort at Beulah to Castell Collen, near Llandrindod Wells and then on to Caersŵs. The road north from Llanio led to a fort at Trawscoed on the River Ystwyth south-east of Aberystwyth. Although the full course of this road is not known it will have continued to a newly discovered fort at Pen Llwyn and then on to Pennal on the Dovey estuary. Roads must have run east to link these forts to those north of Castell Collen, but we know little of them. It is our lack of knowledge rather than Roman idiosyncrasy which is responsible for the fort at Cae Gaer appearing to stand in isolation between Pen Llwyn and Caersŵs. A similar explanation must account for another isolated fort recently discovered at Colwyn Castle to the south-east of Castell Collen.

Forts in north Wales

All the forts listed so far were probably under the command of the Second Augustan Legion at Caerleon, but at some point in mid-Wales control passed to the Twentieth Valeria Victrix in Chester. Caersŵs and the forts to the north of it, possibly including Pennal, formed part of the northern command. The forts at Forden Gaer, near Montgomery, and Caersŵs guarded the road running west from Wroxeter along the Severn valley.

Two roads ran from Chester. The first was along the north coast of Wales, generally keeping rather further inland than its modern successor. No forts are known at its eastern end, although some probably existed. Not until it crosses the valley of the River Conwy do we find a fort at Caerhun. From there the road continued to Caernarfon, where there was an important military site. Another route ran inland from Caerhun following the Conwy valley before turning to cross to the Llugwy valley and a fort at

Bryn-y-gefeiliau, near Capel Curig. From there it continued to the south-west probably as far as Pennal, although the course of its final section is still not completely known. By it, on a bleak hilltop in the Vale of Ffestiniog is the fort of Tomen-y-mur, one of the most interesting Roman sites in Wales, and one of the most exposed. A road must have linked Tomen-y-mur and Caer Gai, although the main approach to the fort at Caer Gai was by way of a road running across north Wales from Chester to the Mawddach estuary. Another possible fort on this road is at Ruthin, and others may still be found. Two forts are known at Llanfor at the north-eastern end of Lake Bala, one of which is unusual in having a polygonal plan, but their date is uncertain. One or both could relate to the conquest period, for they are probably too close to the small fort at Caer Gai to be contemporary. A road must have led due south from Caernarfon, for there is a small fort at Pen Llystyn near Bryncir, at the eastern end of the Llŷn peninsula, placed where it could keep an eye on the inhabitants of the hillforts and hut groups on the peninsula. Where the road went from there is not clear, but it may have followed a circuitous route to Tomen-y-mur.

This concentration of forts in the north-west of Wales probably reflects the centre of Ordovician opposition, and some of them were probably built by Agricola rather than his predecessor Frontinus. The more easterly parts of the tribe, who were probably the majority, had had more experience of the Roman army and may have been more ready to accept Roman government.

These forts are supplemented by a number of smaller fortlets which probably provided strong points between the more widely spaced forts, although there is no regularity in their distribution as it is known at present. Several lie on the road from Llandovery to Castell Collen, where there are also some very small fortlets which probably acted as signal stations.

Once completed this network would have given the Roman army a formidable system of control over the native population of Wales, and with its many garrisons and continuous patrols it would have made revolt a difficult and dangerous ambition. From now on the Romans could consider the Welsh tribes as subdued, and concentrate on introducing them to the Roman way of life. Once that was done, and the benefits of Romanization appreciated, the Roman government would have hoped to close the forts and let civilian government take over – a hope which, as we shall see, was only partially fulfilled.

5 The Legionary Fortress at Caerleon

The legionary fortresses of Britain

For its size Roman Britain retained a surprisingly large military garrison. Its core was formed by three legions in fortresses at Caerleon (Isca, garrisoned by Legio II Augusta), Chester (Deva, garrisoned by Legio XX Valeria Victrix) and York (Eburacum, garrisoned from early in the second century by Legio VI Victrix). The XX Valeria at Chester was responsible for the north of Wales and the southern Pennines where the majority of its auxiliaries were based. The II Augusta at Caerleon was rather different, for while the stationing of a legion there had made strategic sense in the first century, by the middle of the second century it was in an area remote from any obvious military threat and was responsible for no more than a handful of auxiliary units stationed in south and mid-Wales. Its continued existence is probably explained by the fact that it formed a strategic reserve which was sufficiently distant from the other legions to reduce greatly the chance of their combining in rebellion. In reality many of the men in this legion spent much of the second century in the north of Britain, where they helped to build Hadrian's Wall and its short-lived successor, the Antonine Wall, although most probably returned to Caerleon for the winter. But the fortress remained the legion's main administrative centre. The same situation applied to the legion at Chester, but the retention of more forts in the Pennines meant that it had a greater military role in the area.

Of these three legionary fortresses, Caerleon is the only one which does not lie under a modern city, and the only one where the remains of a number of excavated buildings can be seen.

The plan of the fortress

The fortress at Caerleon was founded in the mid-seventies to replace the by then derelict base at Usk (Chapter 4). It has the normal playing-card shape, with an area of 20.5 hectares (50.6 acres), which was more or less normal for a fortress of that date. When it was first built most of the internal buildings were of

Parade Ground

Baths

Amphitheatre

ISCA

Baths

Roman detail, known
Roman detail, presumed

Plan of the legionary fortress at Caerleon. The headquarters building is in the centre of the site with the commander's house behind it.

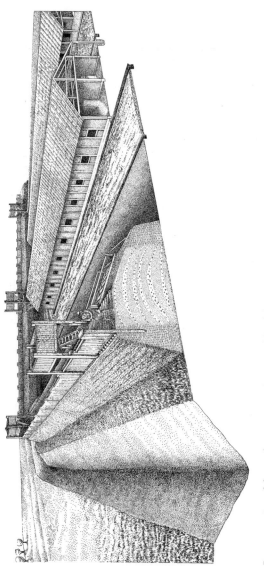

Reconstruction of the north-west corner (Prysg Field) of the legionary fortress at Caerleon soon after its construction in c.AD 75, showing the earth and timber defences and the timber barrack blocks. (Drawn by Howard Mason)

wood. The defences consisted of a ditch in front of an earth bank which was reinforced with turves at back and front and had timber-framed towers set at intervals of 100 Roman feet (97 English feet or 29.6 metres) along it, with large wooden gatehouses in each of the four sides. All of these were rebuilt in stone and a stone wall inserted into the front of the rampart in the early years of the second century.

The interior of the fortress had the usual T-shaped arrangement of main roads with the road forming the stem of the T (the *via praetoria*) running from the south-east gate which faced the river and through which much of the traffic entered the fortress. The head of the T was formed by a road (the *via principalis*) running from the north-east gate to the south-west gate, effectively dividing the interior of the fortress into two slightly asymmetrical halves. Minor roads divided these areas into separate blocks or *insulae*. Even in the timber phase the major roads were lined with colonnades, a refinement which was derived ultimately from the cities of the Mediterranean region.

With the exception of the great bath building, the legionary headquarters (*principia*) and one of the workshops, the main buildings were built of timber. The fact that they were rebuilt in stone in the second century means that the remains of the timber are often difficult to detect, and details are only known from relatively recent excavations. We know that there were changes to some of the minor buildings when they were rebuilt in stone, but the more important ones would have been too large to be re-located without totally changing the plan of the fortress, and we may assume that the stone versions reflect the position and probably largely the plans of their timber predecessors.

All legionary fortresses built at this time have a degree of similarity for the same types of buildings were required by all legions, although there is a degree of flexibility in their positions within the fortress. The headquarters building (*principia*), which was always at the centre of a fortress, consisted of a great basilical hall of almost cathedral-like proportions, open at the front where it faced a large courtyard with ranges of rooms on the other three sides. There was a row of rooms at the back of the hall, most of which were probably offices, but the central one was where the legionary standards were displayed. This hall was the symbolic heart of the legion. Immediately behind it stood the *praetorium*, the residence of the legionary commander, a Roman of the highest social class, usually in his early thirties, who probably had his wife and family with him

34

Photograph of an inscription from Caerleon recording the dedication of a major building under the Emperor Trajan (Nerva Trajan Augustus, son of the deified Nerva etc.) in AD 100.

as well as numerous slaves and servants. The details of the building are imperfectly known, but it consisted of ranges of rooms arranged around a large oval courtyard, on the south-east side of which was a basilical hall where the commander could receive native aristocrats with all the pomp and ceremony which his rank and position required. Each of his senior officers, mostly wealthy young men, had his own house on the southern side of the *via principalis*.

A Roman legion was capable of producing and repairing much of its own equipment, and great workshops (*fabricae*) are found in all fortresses. At Caerleon there are *fabricae* on each side of the commander's house, while a building on the eastern side of the headquarters building, partially excavated early in the last century, may be another. Two other major buildings are known within the fortress: a hospital, consisting of a series of corridors and rooms arranged around a large central courtyard, stood on the south-eastern side of the fortress, with a large bath building on its western side.

The legionary bathhouse

Roman baths were of the type which we call 'Turkish baths', a series of rooms progressively increasing in heat, of which the last and hottest was heavy with steam from an open pool of near boiling water. Such baths were the most essential luxury of the Roman world and without them life would have been regarded as almost unbearable by any Roman. For that reason they were a prime requirement in all forts and fortresses, and the 5,000 men in the legionary fortress needed a very large bathhouse. The main part of the building lay to the south of the *via principalis*, behind the officers' houses, but it was fronted by a basilical hall which extended as far as the main road. This hall, which may not have been completed, was designed to provide a covered area, sheltered from the vagaries of the Welsh climate, where the men could relax. On one side of the building was a large courtyard for exercise, with a covered colonnade around its sides and a long pool at its centre where the hardier bathers could swim. The main bath building consisted of three huge vaulted halls built of stone and concrete to reduce the risk of fire. Such baths were the only buildings which could never be built of wood and even in the earliest fortresses, such as Usk or Exeter, we find stone bath buildings. The first of the halls, that adjacent to the basilical hall, was the cold room (*frigidarium*) where the men undressed. In it were pools of cold water for the bathers to cool themselves. Then came two rooms with the under-floor heating system (hypocausts) which is a characteristic feature of Roman bathhouses. The first was the warm room (*tepidarium*), the second the hot, steam room (*caldarium*) where the bathers usually wore slippers to protect their feet from the painfully hot floor. All the various elements of the baths are known from excavation, but only parts of the courtyard, swimming pool and cold room have been totally excavated and are now displayed to the public.

One other important group of buildings which must have existed but which have not been located at Caerleon are the granaries. We know from other fortresses such as Chester that there were at least six and probably eight massive granaries with raised floors and strongly buttressed walls, each capable of holding several hundred tons of grain. Ideally all Roman forts had a year's reserve of grain, and a fortress such as Caerleon would have needed large stores of preserved meat, wine and olive oil as well.

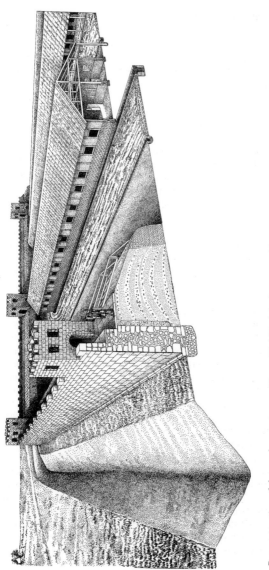

Reconstruction of the north-west corner (Prysg Field) of the legionary fortress at Caerleon in the mid-second century, showing the stone defences and half-timbered barrack blocks. (Drawn by Howard Mason)

Barracks

The remainder of the interior was occupied by the rows of barrack blocks. Those to the west of the headquarters were for the first cohort, the most highly experienced troops in the legion, whose centurions were each responsible for two centuries of men and who had correspondingly large houses. A group of more normal barrack blocks are displayed in the north-western corner of the fortress (Prysg Field), but only that closest to the rampart is original, the others, which lie at a higher level, being modern reconstructions. Each barrack consists of a long row of paired rooms (*contubernia*), the back ones being slightly larger than the front ones. They were fronted by a veranda which protected the

Life in the barracks
A century should have had 100 men in it but, quite illogically, it actually contained 80, divided into ten *contubernia,* a term deriving from the tent which the same group of men shared in the field. It is something of a surprise, therefore, to find that each barrack block at Caerleon actually has twelve *contubernia.* The function of the spare rooms is uncertain. They could have held new recruits undergoing training and not yet assigned a place in a century, or stores, or even the personal slaves which inscriptions tell us were owned by some legionaries. It is generally assumed that the soldiers kept their personal equipment in the front room of their *contubernium* and slept in the back room, perhaps in bunk beds. Looking at these small rooms it is difficult to believe that eight men could have spent some twenty-five years living in such cramped quarters, but in reality most of them would have done little more than sleep in their barracks, and often probably not even that. We know that many legionaries had common-law wives and families, and we are told by the historian Herodian that from the end of the second century they were allowed to live with them outside the fortress. Although most of the barracks were rebuilt with stone footings at intervals during the second century, their narrow walls suggest that they carried little weight and the superstructure may have been of wood or wattle and daub.

men when they went from one *contubernium* to another. The centurion's quarters lay at one end of the block, occupying almost one-third of its total length – a very visible reminder of the importance of the centurion in the military hierarchy. Each centurion probably had his own small staff as well as personal slaves, all of whom were accommodated in his quarters.

A road ran around the perimeter of the fortress, giving access to the defences in the event of an attack. In the area of the Prysg Field between the corner tower and the north-west gate, the space between this road and the fortress wall on the north side was filled with a jumble of stores and workshops, with cookhouses and the clay and stone ovens which the soldiers used for baking their bread on the west side. Cooking in the confined space of barracks was impractical and dangerous. Near the corner of the fortress is a large latrine, its sewer flushed by water from a tank.

The amphitheatre

Two structures were too big to be placed in the defended area, the parade ground and the amphitheatre. Both were on the western side of the fortress, the parade ground being no more than a large open area to the north of the west gate, with the amphitheatre to its south. The amphitheatre, which was built late in the first century, has a sunken arena which provided the earth for the seating banks which were revetted at back and front with stone walls. The inner wall still retains patches of the smooth mortar facing which helped to prevent hunted animals climbing up into the seating. As usual the main entrances into the arena are on the main axis but there are six additional entrances which gave access both to the seating and to the arena. These entrances opened onto passages which sloped down to stairs leading to the seating from where a second stair led down into the arena. The entrances on the shorter axis had double stairs leading to a box for important spectators, below which was a small room opening into the arena. Most amphitheatres do not have access from the seating into the arena, for few spectators actually wanted to join in the bloody events, much as they enjoyed watching them. But such entrances are normal in military amphitheatres; they can also be seen in the Chester amphitheatre, for example. The explanation lies in the fact that they were built for the legions and were designed for training the men as well as for entertainment. Watched by the rest of the legion, units would move into the arena to perform drills or manœuvres before being replaced by another group. The discovery of a series of holes in which large posts were set in the banks around the arena suggests that the seating was carried on a massive wooden superstructure of the type shown in an amphitheatre depicted on Trajan's Column in Rome.

Originally the tunnels were vaulted which allowed the seating to continue unbroken around the arena. Unfortunately this arrangement had one major fault, for the fact that the passages sloped down from their entrances meant that water running into the tunnels was dammed by the stairs at their ends, with the result that for large parts of the year spectators had to wade through pools of stagnant water to reach their seats. Somewhat surprisingly this arrangement continued for over a hundred years until around 210–20 when the whole amphitheatre was refurbished and the floors of the tunnels levelled. Unfortunately, the vaulted roofs were parallel with the floor which meant that now there was insufficient headroom at the foot of the stairs for the spectators to get to their seats, a problem which could only be solved by removing the roofs from the tunnels.

The amphitheatre outside the fortress at Chester was similar in most respects to that at Caerleon, although the excavators thought that it was built entirely of stone rather than having a wooden superstructure as at Caerleon. Where the two differed, however, was in the fact that the stone arena at Chester had been preceded by a smaller timber-built amphitheatre. The assumption is that this was the work of the Second Legion Adiutrix which built the fortress in the mid-seventies, and that it was rebuilt in stone by the Twentieth Legion which moved to Chester in c.AD 86.

The amphitheatres at both Caerleon and Chester were built within a few metres of the fortress wall, so close indeed that their huge bulk must have loomed over the fortress defences. If an enemy had succeeded in getting control of the amphitheatre it would have given them total command of the interior of the fortress. Few things show more clearly the arrogant confidence of the Roman army of the late first century; to them it was inconceivable that an enemy would dare to attack a legionary fortress, and, as far as Britain was concerned, they were probably right.

Roman legionaries of the first and second centuries were recruited mainly in the more Romanized provinces, and gladiatorial shows and wild beast hunts would have been among their favourite amusements. We know relatively little of the type of entertainment which would have been seen in British arenas, but elaborate programmes with wild beast hunts and large numbers of gladiators would have been rare at minor venues such as Caerleon. We have some evidence for troops of travelling gladiators, probably working with actors and actresses, and Caerleon may have been on their itinerary, but gladiators were a valuable investment and it is unlikely that they would have fought to the death in Caerleon. The staple entertainment is more likely to have been wild beast hunts and bull- or bear-baiting. It is just possible, however, that the arena may have been the scene of the martyr-dom of two Christians in the mid-third century, for Gildas, writing in the sixth century, records the execution of Aaron and Julius, who came from the 'city of the legions', which is thought to refer to Caerleon rather than Chester or York, but whether they died in the arena or outside the fortress we do not know.

The fact that Caerleon stands on the River Usk at a point which could be reached by sea-going vessels was no accident. In the ancient world it was far cheaper to carry goods by ship than overland, and wherever possible legionary fortresses were placed on navigable rivers, as was York, or on estuaries, as were Caerleon and Chester. The advantages of being able to bring bulky goods such as building materials or grain to the fortress by water is obvious, and excavations have confirmed the existence of docks on the Usk immediately outside the fortress.

Life in the fortress

It is not always appreciated that the fortress of Caerleon was the centre of a sprawling town (*canabae*) which provided for the requirements of the legionaries when they were off duty, and where discharged legionaries and their families often chose to live. By civilian standards a Roman legionary was well paid, and a legion would have been a magnet to entrepreneurs of every kind. Before the early years of the third century serving soldiers were not allowed to marry, but it was natural that many of them formed permanent relationships with local women, some of whom were themselves probably the children of legionaries. From the end of the second century legionaries were allowed to live with their families, with the result that the fortress became closely integrated into a complex society which was wholly dependent on the legion for its existence. The officers often had their families with them,

41

and they would certainly have had slaves and servants, as would most of the centurions and some of the legionaries. Given the fact that many of the men had families outside the fortress, it is likely that the division between the fortress and its surrounding suburbs was highly flexible, with civilians as free to go into the fortress, to use the baths perhaps, as the soldiers were to go out of it.

Excavations outside the fortress have cast some light on the buildings around it, but the best sources of information are the

The living and the dead

One of the largest groups of inscriptions are tombstones, of which the most interesting come from Great Bulmore, a suburb of the fortress a short way upstream, where a number of legionary veterans and their families lived. A Roman legionary usually enlisted in his late teens and served for twenty-five years, by which time many must have formed local connections and lost touch with their original homelands. For them retirement close to the fortress which had been their home for so many years was an obvious choice. Many tombstones are distinctly formulaic, giving the names of the person commemorated and the person who erected the stone. In the case of a soldier, serving or retired, they usually give the details of the unit, here '*Legio II Augusta*', and their age at death. If they died while still on active service, the number of years which they had served when they died is also given. What they do not give is the year of their death, a fact which makes it extremely difficult to date such tombstones. The great majority of the military tombstones were erected by the men's wives or children. Life in the ancient world was relatively short, but enlistment in the army, with its regime of hard exercise, plentiful food and a good medical service, often led to the men living to a good age. Even so, Julius Valens who died at the age of a hundred was exceptional by any standard. His wife lived to be seventy-five, as her own tombstone records. Interestingly few men are said to have died on active service. Only one, who is commemorated with his mother on her tombstone, is said to have died on the 'German Expedition', a reminder that parts of the legion could be sent to serve in wars elsewhere in the Empire.

various inscriptions found there and now displayed in Caerleon Museum. Many of them refer to building projects, usually giving the name of the emperor or emperors under whom the work was done. But others are more personal. Some are concerned with religious matters, and we find the commander of the legion restoring a Temple of Diana, while others celebrate Classical deities such as Mercury, or the eastern gods Jupiter Dolichenus and Mithras – the last a god who was highly favoured by officers (Chapter 10). What are lacking are inscriptions to native British deities, a significant contrast to the situation in the cities or even in auxiliary forts.

6 The Forts

By the end of the first century Roman forts were largely standardized in plan. Although many of the forts of Wales have been partially excavated, in most cases the work was insufficient to reveal much of their plan, while in others it was done at a time when archaeologists were incapable of elucidating the complex histories of such sites.

We know scarcely anything of the internal details of the forts built before Frontinus. All that we can say is that they contained wooden buildings and were enclosed by earth banks fronted by one or more ditches, with timber interval towers and gatehouses. The forts which replaced them in the seventies were initially built in the same way, although only at Pen Llystyn, which was never rebuilt in stone, do we have a reasonably complete plan. In the main early excavators had great difficulty in detecting the remains of timber buildings, and while their reports show that such buildings had existed, they could not work out the details of their plans. Unfortunately the most extensive excavations on Roman forts in Wales were undertaken before the Second World War. More recent work on sites such as Cardiff, Castell Collen, Neath, Loughor and Caernarfon has been on a more limited scale and is of particular value in helping to reveal their development and the changes which took place over time. Several early excavations, notably those at Brecon Gaer, Caersŵs and Castell Collen, concentrated on the stone buildings in the central range, the headquarters building, the commanding officer's house and the granaries, but in a few others (Caerhun, Caernarfon and Gelligaer) some of the barracks and ancillary buildings were also excavated.

The garrisons

All these forts were garrisoned by auxiliary units, but, in the absence of inscriptions, identification of the type of unit from the plan of the fort is difficult, indeed usually impossible. In a few cases we have inscriptions naming the garrison, but even then it is unlikely to have been there throughout the life of the fort.

Fortunately some diplomas engraved on bronze survive. These were legal documents issued to auxiliary soldiers when they were discharged, and the ones relevant to Wales list the auxiliary units allied to the legions at Caerleon and Chester in the opening years of the second century. We may assume that all the former were based in south Wales, but the Chester command covered the southern Pennines as well as north Wales. The figures are:

	Caerleon	Chester
Units of 480 Cavalry	4	4
ala quingenariae		
Units of 800 infantry and 240 cavalry	1	1
cohors milliaria equitata		
Units of 1,000 infantry	1	0
cohors milliaria peditata		
Units of 360 infantry and 120 cavalry	5	8
cohortes quingenariae equitatae		
Units of 480 infantry	4	3
cohortes quinegenariae peditatae		

From this we can calculate that the auxiliary garrison of south Wales was around 8,000, of whom one-third were cavalry, with the total for the whole of Wales being in the region of 12,000 men. Of these we know from inscriptions that at some time one of the 480-strong cavalry units, the *ala Hispanorum Vettonum civium Romanum*, was at Brecon Gaer; a smaller mixed cavalry and infantry unit, the *cohors II Asturum*, at Llanio; and a similar unit, *cohors I Nerviorum*, at Caer Gai, but beyond that we cannot safely go. The first two originated in Spain, the third in north-west Gaul. Attempts to identify the type of unit based in a fort by relating the number of men to the size of the fort usually fail on the differing requirements of infantry and cavalry soldiers, and on the fact that similar units need not have built forts of equal size. This applies even to the legions, for while the legions at Chester and Caerleon had the same number of men, the fortress at Chester was some 20 per cent larger than that at Caerleon.

Fort plans

Most of the forts vary only slightly in size. A small group (Brecon Gaer, Caersŵs and Forden Gaer) with areas of 3.1 hectares (7.6

acres) were notably larger than the rest where the norm was between 2.0 and 2.4 hectares (5–6 acres). All were very similar in their basic arrangements, and all were essentially miniature versions of the legionary fortresses from which their plan ultimately derived. Rectangular in outline, with gates in each of the four sides, they were divided into two unequal halves by a road running across the fort between two of the gates (the *via principalis*). On

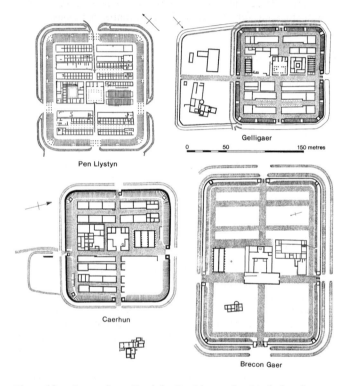

Pen Llystyn

Gelligaer

0   50   150 metres

Caerhun

Brecon Gaer

Plans of four Roman forts. Top left: Pen Llystyn showing the late first-century timber buildings. Top right: Gelligaer showing the stone buildings of the early second-century fort with the bathhouse in an annexe. Bottom left: Caerhun showing the second-century stone buildings with the bathhouse outside the fort. Bottom right: Brecon Gaer showing the second-century stone buildings at the centre of the fort and the late bathhouse.

this road, facing the main gate, were the most important buildings, the headquarters (*principia*) at the centre, with the commanding officer's house (*praetorium*) on one side and the granaries (*horrea*), which could hold enough grain to feed the garrison for a year, on the other. On the opposite side of the road, and in the area behind the main buildings, were barracks and other structures which were probably workshops and stables. Around the perimeter of the fort, just behind the defences, were the ovens in which the men baked their bread, set as far as possible from the timber buildings.

The soldiers' accommodation

Life in an auxiliary fort was probably very similar to that in a legionary fortress (Chapter 5), and the arrangement of the barracks was not dissimilar, although an auxiliary *contubernium* often had only a single room. Some early excavators, including those at Gelligaer, Caernarfon and Caerhun, failed to detect wooden internal divisions within the barrack blocks. Cavalry units were divided into *turmae* (troops or squadrons) rather than centuries, each probably containing thirty men, but how they were divided among the barracks is far from clear. Nor is it known how many of their mounts were stabled inside the fort.

Rebuilding in stone

Building forts in earth and timber was quick, but it meant that the buildings had a relatively short life. For forts built in the aftermath of campaigns this was not a problem, but where they were intended to last for generations stone had obvious advantages, and so we begin to find that, from the beginning of the second century, key buildings were being rebuilt in stone. In fact almost all the forts erected in the seventies show this development, apart from Pen Llystyn which was demolished before rebuilding began. Priority was given to the defences, with stone walls and gates being added to the existing earth banks, and to rebuilding the central range of buildings (the headquarters building, the commanding officer's house and the granaries). In several cases (Brecon Gaer, Caersŵs and Castell Collen) this appears to be all that was done, with the barracks continuing to be built of wood which was replaced when necessary. In a few forts such as Caerhun and

Caernarfon, all the internal buildings were replaced in stone, although the work was probably spread over many years. Gelligaer was unusual in having the stone fort built just outside its late first-century predecessor. An inscription from the site shows that the new fort was built in the first decade of the second century. We know from documentary sources that many of the soldiers were trained in a craft, and most of the construction work would have been done by the unit itself, if necessary with some help from the legionaries. No doubt the commanders of these units regarded this work as good practice for their men and as an effective way of keeping them busy and physically active.

Outside the fort would be the bathhouse, sometimes set in an enclosure attached to the fort as at Gelligaer or Bryn-y-gefeiliau. It was unusual for a bathhouse to be built inside a fort, and where we do find it, as at Caernarfon and Brecon Gaer, it probably indicates that it was erected at a late date when the fort held a reduced garrison. A most unusual luxury at Tomen-y-mur was a small amphitheatre built close to the fort; although not unique, such arenas are great rarities at auxiliary forts.

We know from inscriptions found in forts elsewhere in Britain that the garrisons of forts were changed at surprisingly frequent intervals, presumably in response to local requirements and the logistical demands of the province, and this is probably the explanation of the structural changes which we see in many of the Welsh forts. It may explain the unusual position of some of the main buildings at Brecon Gaer, while in at least three cases (Castell Collen, Tomen-y-mur and Caerau) the internal area was reduced by building a new wall to cut off one end of the fort. In such cases there is little doubt that a smaller unit had moved in and adapted its new base to suit its own requirements.

Most of these forts, certainly those which were occupied for any length of time, saw a civilian settlement develop outside their walls. Such settlements, which are usually known by their Latin name, *vici* – or *vicus* in the singular – are discussed more fully in Chapter 9.

7 Changing the System: The Beginning of Civilian Government

Once Wales was conquered the Romans were able to begin the processes designed to lead the tribes to self-government and allow the military garrisons to be withdrawn. To the Romans the normal political unit was the city state, where the city was surrounded and largely supported by its own territory; a system in which the city was always pre-eminent. Under this system most aspects of local government could be left to the natives, under the watchful eye of the Roman governor, while Rome retained control of military and international matters, and most aspects of taxation.

The problem of Wales

Unfortunately the foundation of this scheme was missing over much of barbarian Europe which lacked what the Romans would have regarded as real cities. Instead there was a tribal structure with many simple urban centres, such as hillforts, all of more or less equal status. The Romans had already faced this problem on the Continent and had developed a solution which was to treat the tribe itself, both the people and the territory, as if it was a city. In legal terms (and the Romans preferred such things to be legally defined) it was a *civitates peregrinae* – a self-governing community consisting of the citizens of the city, in this case a rather theoretical one. With time and firm encouragement cities would develop in the tribal areas, but when they did they were not normally made independent of the tribe.

Self-government

At first tribal self-government was only possible in those areas which had been under Roman control for some years, the Marches and parts of south-east Wales – areas which had become familiar with Roman ideas and customs. The military system created by Frontinus involved the removal of most of the troops from those areas, but for the time being, the rest of Wales remained under

The governors of Britain

Although Britain was not among the richest provinces in the Roman Empire, the fact that it had a large military garrison made it one of the more important ones. Legally the Roman emperor himself was the governor of the province, as he was of all provinces which had a large military garrison, but in reality he appointed a deputy to do the work. Such men, whose official title was *Legatus Augusti pro praetore*, were successful and experienced men who were senior members of the Senate and regarded by the emperor as both able and loyal.

To prepare them for such positions they had held a series of administrative and military offices, at fixed intervals holding one of the traditional offices of Rome necessary to qualify them for the next series of posts. They began their training at eighteen with a minor administrative post followed by appointment as an officer in a legion (military tribune). If they made a success of that they were appointed as a *quaestor* and became Roman senators at about the age of twenty-four. After more administrative posts the next hurdle, the *praetorship*, came when they were in their late twenties, followed by a legionary command, and then the governorship of a minor province with few or no troops in it. Then they would hope for the great honour, the consulship, by then little more than a title, but originally the most powerful post in the Roman Republic. Once a man had held the consulship he was marked out for high office. If destined for a major military province such as Britain he might govern another, less important province first. Such men would have acquired extensive experience in all aspects of military and provincial administration, for the governor of a province was the commander of the army, head of the administration (save for financial affairs), and the supreme legal officer with the power of life and death over the provincials.

Most governors served for three years and for about half of them Britain was the culmination of their career, but others rose to still greater heights, further consulships and perhaps ultimately the governorship of the provinces of Africa or Asia.

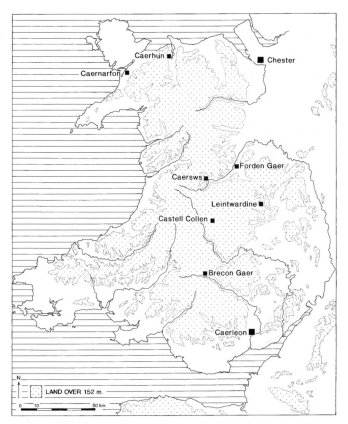

Roman forts in Wales which were still in use in the mid-second century.

military control, although the long-term aim remained the creation of self-government in all areas.

In one respect the plan worked well, for over the next seventy or so years it was possible to close most of the forts in Wales. A small number went quite soon, but the first large programme of closures came with the construction of Hadrian's Wall in the 120s when auxiliary units were required for the new forts on the northern frontier. This was followed in the 140s by the removal of most of

51

the remaining troops as a result of reoccupation of southern Scotland by Antoninus Pius. From then on only a handful of Welsh forts were still occupied. In the south the fort at Cardiff was certainly retained, a fact which probably reflected its importance as a harbour, for it lay in one of the most Romanized parts of Wales and there can have been no local threat. Both Loughor and Neath may have been occupied in the middle years of the second century, but the details are obscure and it is possible that the occupation of the forts was not military. In mid-Wales Brecon Gaer and Castell Collen were retained, both key sites in their areas, while just over the English border a new fort was built at Leintwardine to replace an earlier one on a slightly different site. Further north the importance of the upper Severn valley explains the retention of the forts at Forden Gaer and Caersŵs. On the north coast there were garrisons at Caerhun, which controlled the Conwy valley, and Caernarfon. The maintenance of Caernarfon is explained by the need to control the Menai Straits and access to Anglesey with its rich mineral resources.

Military control

Such an arrangement makes little military sense, for the forts are too dispersed to control a hostile population. Indeed, in the event of trouble, they would have been annihilated before news of the danger even reached the legionary commanders. The fact that the Romans were able to close the other forts makes it clear that by the middle of the second century the Welsh tribes had accepted Roman rule. But seen in the context of the progress of Romanization in Wales and the development of a system of civilian government, the system is more meaningful. Only in the south had Romanization really taken hold with the development of Caerwent and Carmarthen as the tribal capitals of the Silures and Demetae respectively. The result was that the greater part of mid and north Wales lacked a normal civilian administration, not because the Romans did not want one but because the conditions, with small and divided populations living in a rugged landscape where communications were difficult, militated against the development of the towns necessary for the Roman system to function. But the Roman government could not abandon those areas; that would have invited trouble, and in any case they wanted the tax revenue from them and to exploit the mineral resources of north and west Wales. Equally importantly, these areas were excellent recruiting grounds for the auxiliary units, producing as they did men who were used to hard physical work.

Under these circumstances the choice of forts which were retained makes good sense for they provided a framework for the Roman administration in an area which lacked any kind of town.

8 The Cities of Wales

As we saw in Chapter 7, the city state was alien to most of the barbarian world including Britain, but the Romans had faced the problem in Gaul and other provinces many years before the conquest of Britain, and they had devised a simple solution, treating the entire tribe as if it was a city.

City administration

A city such as Caerwent was administered by a council (the *ordo*), modelled on the Senate of Rome, consisting of around 100 men (*decurions*) who were probably drawn initially from the tribal nobility. Routine administration was the responsibility of four magistrates, two senior and two junior, who also presided in the tribal law courts. The citizens of the tribe probably participated in the system by electing the junior magistrates who became decurions when their term of office ended; this was the main way of renewing the council. The system had an element of democracy, but it was strictly limited for all councillors had to pass a property qualification, which was high, and men who were not citizens of the town, and all women, were excluded from the process. The prestige of being a decurion was tempered by the fact that they were responsible for collecting the tribal taxes and, in the event of a deficit, had to make it up from their own resources.

Obviously the Romans hoped that cities would develop, and they encouraged such development, but any cities which did appear did not have the same independent legal standing as the cities of the Mediterranean region, or even the *colonia* of Britain such as Colchester or Gloucester. There the land belonged to the city; in Britain it was the other way round. The cities which developed and became the administrative centres of the British tribes are often referred to as tribal capitals, but they did not have the independent status of a modern capital city. This is why the 'Paulinus stone' from Caerwent was erected by order of the

'Council of the Republic of the Silures' (the legal name of the tribe) and not by the council of the City of Caerwent as would have been the case in the Mediterranean provinces.

All true Romans regarded the city as the centre of civilized life. It was there that you found the social amenities which made life worth living, the shops, the taverns, the baths, the arenas and theatres and, above all, society. And this, of course, was the model of civilized life which was presented to the Britons. For the native nobility to be accepted and rewarded by the Romans they had to accept Roman ideas, and the city was at the centre of those ideas.

The basic economic system of production and exchange played a major part in the development of cities in Roman Britain. They were the places where agricultural produce could be sold and the manufactured and imported goods, which became increasingly common and varied as the Roman system developed, bought. This process was given an immense impetus by the construction of the extensive road system which linked key points throughout the province. Without a viable commercial infrastructure the town was an alien creation brought into existence for a political purpose and doomed to inevitable failure.

Cities of Wales

Most of the tribes of England developed at least one city which acted as an administrative centre, but only the Demetae and Silures did this in Wales. The Ordovices were almost unique, outside the military zone of northern England, in not having a tribal city, although there were a few large villages on their eastern fringes, Whitchurch (Mediolanum) being the most notable. The major city of the northern Marches was Wroxeter, the tribal city of the Cornovii, and there can be little doubt that it was the centre of the economic life of much of the mid and northern Marches.

The reasons why so few cities developed in Wales are relatively simple: the hilly, often mountainous, terrain made communications difficult and divided the population into small communities which were not large enough to generate the economic momentum required for a town to develop. Agriculture was the basis of most wealth in the ancient world, with mining and manufactured goods coming a long way behind. Unfortunately, although parts of mid and north Wales had good agricultural potential, any surplus which they produced was useless unless it could be brought to

Photograph of the 'Paulinus Stone': the base of a statue of Tiberius Claudius Paulinus, governor of Britannia Inferior, erected by the 'Republic of the Silures' at Caerwent in the third century.

The Paulinus stone

Tiberio Claudio Paulino legato legionis II Augustae proconsuli provinciae Narbonensis legato Augusti pro praetore provinciae Lugudunensis ex decreto ordinis respublica civitatis Silurum

To Tiberius Claudius Paulinus, legate of the Second Legion Augusta, proconsul of the province of Narbonensis, emperor's propraetorian legate of the province of Lugudunensis, by decree of the council, the Republic (tribe) of the Silures set this up.

This famous inscription, one of the most important from Roman Britain, is kept in the porch of the village church. Originally it was the base for a statue of Tiberius Claudius Paulinus, a distinguished Roman official of the early third century, who had become the patron of the citizens of Caerwent. In common with most honorific inscriptions it lists his more important offices in the order in which he had held them. The first of these explains his interest in Caerwent, for early in his career he had commanded the Second Augustan Legion at Caerleon, and it was then that he would have come to know Caerwent and its citizens. After leaving Caerleon he became governor of the wealthy province of Gallia Narbonensis (modern Provence), and then of Gallia Lugudunensis, which was the largest province in Gaul. We know from other inscriptions that he returned to Britain as governor of Britannia Inferior (Lower Britain), as the northern part of Britain was known from the beginning of the third century, and his statue was probably erected when the citizens of Caerwent heard that he was returning to Britain. It was important for provincial cities to have patrons in high places who would support their interests in the nepotistic élite which ran the Roman Empire, and the nobility of the Silures had no intention of losing Paulinus' favour if the cost of a statue would ensure its continuance.

The fact that the inscription records that the statue was erected 'by decree of the council, the Republic [i.e. tribe] of the Silures' (*ordinis respublica civitatis Silurum*) confirms that it was the tribe and not the city which was the administrative authority.

market, and the cities which would have provided such markets were too far away for this to be commercially viable. Only on the south coast of Wales were economic conditions more favourable and it is here that we find Caerwent and Carmarthen, the only cities which developed in Wales.

Caerwent (Venta Silurum)

By Continental, or even English, standards Caerwent was a very small city. When, relatively late in its history, it was given defensive walls they enclosed no more than 18 hectares (44 acres). But small as it was, it was a city and it contained most of the major buildings necessary for a city to function.

The origins of the city

The origins of Caerwent are obscure. Most Romano-British cities either grew out of existing native centres or were built on the land originally occupied by Roman forts. However, there is no evidence for a pre-Roman settlement at Caerwent, nor is there much evidence for a Roman fort there, although it is not impossible that one existed in the area. Caerwent occupied a key position where the road running inland from an important crossing of the Severn estuary met the main east–west road through south Wales, and a fort at such a site would not be unlikely. The discovery of an early pottery kiln, producing types of pots which might be expected in an early military context, below the later houses at Pound Lane in the centre of the city may be evidence of such a fort.

In the early years of the conquest the whole territory of the Silures was under military control. We do not know with certainty when the tribe was thought to be sufficiently pacified, and its nobility suitably Romanized, for it to have been accorded self-government, but the construction of the forum and basilica, the physical representation of self-government, was begun in the early years of the second century, a time when such buildings were constructed in a number of Romano-British tribal capitals. A long inscription from Wroxeter shows that the basilica of that city was built in Hadrian's reign and this must indicate that by then the city had become the centre of a self-governing tribe, in that case the Cornovii. Pottery found under the forum at Caerwent suggests that work on the complex had begun by 120, and this may indicate that the Silures, at the other end of the Marches, had received similar status a few years before Wroxeter.

A Roman city, even one as remote and small as Caerwent, was a centre of a Romanized way of life, and this is reflected in the buildings found within it. The administrative aspects are represented by the forum and basilica, the *mansio* (an inn for travellers on state business), and in the infrastructure of the city, its streets, and when these became necessary, its defences. Religion, which permeated the life of the Roman world, is seen in its native guise in the temples which were dedicated to local deities, but the state religion of Rome had its place in the basilica. Social life was represented by the public baths and, in many cities, by a theatre or

Excavations at Caerwent

The plan of Roman Caerwent is familiar to all students of Roman archaeology. Most of our knowledge of it derives from a series of extensive excavations which took place between 1899 and 1913, supplemented by later work on the defences and some shops and houses. More recently parts of the forum and basilica, the adjacent temple and a shop have been re-excavated. The result is that we have a plan of some two-thirds of the town, but it is a plan which presents many problems. Archaeological techniques were in their infancy when most of Caerwent was dug, and the excavators usually only obtained plans of the final phases of the buildings which they found. Today we know that most of these buildings were probably the product of a long and complex process of development lasting for centuries in many cases. Nor were the early excavators able to give dates to much of what they found, with the result that the overall plan shows buildings of widely varying dates. A further problem is that timber buildings were only rarely detected before the 1930s, and timber was an important building material even in a district as rich in building stone as here. However, if these limitations are borne in mind, the plan which we have remains a valuable source of information.

amphitheatre, although the former certainly did not exist at Caerwent and the latter may not have. All these were public buildings, at least in the sense of being frequented by the public even if they were not all owned by the tribal council, but they existed to serve the members of the tribe, particularly those who lived in the city and who are represented in the archaeological record by the houses and workshops which form the majority of the buildings discovered in the city.

The streets

In common with most of the tribal capitals of Roman Britain, Caerwent had a relatively regular grid of streets dividing the city into twenty roughly equal blocks (*insulae*). A glance at the plan of the city makes it clear that these roads are rather irregular in their layout, and recent excavations have shown that the street grid was not constructed until the late second or early third century; before

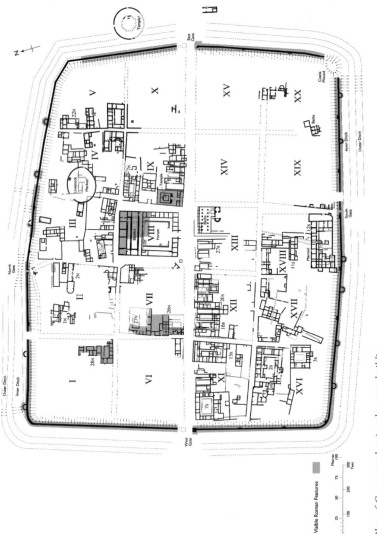

Plan of Caerwent showing the stone buildings.

that the city was dominated by the main road to Caerleon with smaller, and less regular, streets running from it. The streets themselves were constructed of rammed gravel, which grew markedly thicker as time passed and new surfaces were laid down. Like most British cities Caerwent lacked a system of drains and water, and no doubt a great amount of waste simply ran off into side gutters.

Although there is no evidence of a large aqueduct supplying Caerwent with water, the remains of wooden water pipes found at the north gate confirm that fresh water was brought into the city from a nearby spring. This may have been destined for the public baths, or for a drinking fountain near the forum, or both, but most people would have been dependent on water from wells.

The forum and basilica

The forum and basilica complex was the physical and political centre of the city and the tribe, and by the early second century when it was built such buildings had become standardized in plan. One side of the complex was a great basilical hall divided into a nave and aisles by two rows of massive Corinthian columns. With a height of about 20 metres (65 feet) it was the largest civil building in Wales before the coming of the Normans and soared high above the rest of the city. On its southern side was the forum, a large, flagged court surrounded by colonnades with rooms behind them which provided a mixture of offices and prestigious shops. The buildings of the forum probably stood to about half the height of the basilica. Traditionally a forum was a market, and there is no reason to doubt that regular markets were held in the courtyard of the forum at Caerwent.

Entry to the basilica from the forum was through a colonnade fronted by shallow steps. At the ends of the nave were open-fronted rooms, separated from the main hall by a low screen; these were the tribunals where the magistrates sat when they administered justice, and the law which they applied was the traditional law of the tribe. However, their powers were limited in major cases, particularly those involving the death penalty or where there was a clash between local and Roman law, and such cases were usually referred to the provincial governor, who probably undertook an annual progress around the tribal capitals to act as a supreme justice.

The basilicas of the great Continental cities, and perhaps a few of those in Britain, also served as financial centres. But this type of finance is unlikely to have played a large part in the life of Caerwent, and for much of the year the basilica can hardly have been used. At its back, though, was a row of rooms which would have been in more regular use. These were not as lofty as the main hall, but were of similar height to the forum. The central one, which was open-fronted with its floor raised above that of the main hall, was almost certainly the centre of Roman state religion in the city. This took a double form: worship of the state deities of Rome, the Capitoline triad, and of the imperial cult, the worship of those emperors who had been deified by the Roman Senate (Chapter 10). Acceptance of these cults was an act of loyalty that all who lived within the Empire were required to observe, and refusal was not heresy but treason. To the west of the shrine was a larger room which recent excavations have shown to have had raised wooden seating on two sides with a dais on the third. This was the *curia* where the tribal council (the *ordo*) met. The function of the other rooms is not known, but one of them probably held the city's archives. Late in the third century, when the basilica was over a century and a half old, it was extensively rebuilt, possibly as a result of subsidence. Half a century later, around 340, numerous hearths were built within it, suggesting that it had ceased to be an administrative centre and had been converted into workshops. A similar fate befell the basilica of Silchester, Hampshire, at much the same time. Twenty or so years later the great hall was completely demolished. Clearly late Roman Caerwent no longer needed such a hall; a reminder of the fact that the cities of later Roman Britain were very different from those of the years after the conquest.

The public baths

Facing the forum were the public baths, the building which for most people would have been the social centre of the city. Such baths, the predecessors of our 'Turkish' baths, were the most successful of all Roman introductions, and there was scarcely a city in the Empire which did not have its public baths. The fortress baths at Caerleon have been described in Chapter 5, and those at Caerwent had the same basic sequence of cold, warm and hot rooms. The main rooms lie below later buildings and only a small part of the complex could be excavated, but this revealed that they were fronted by a large colonnaded hall similar to the hall of the baths at Caerleon. In the Mediterranean provinces public baths often had open courts for exercise but in Britain a covered hall was a sensible, although relatively rare, replacement; in this case the baths at Caerleon probably formed the model.

A possible amphitheatre

Many British cities had either a theatre or an amphitheatre, although not both. One of the more enigmatic discoveries at Caerwent was a large oval enclosure in the north-western quarter of the city. Its date was not established by the excavators, but the fact that it overlay earlier stone houses and a section of road shows that it was built fairly late in the history of the city. In shape and size it is reminiscent of the arena of an amphitheatre, and that was how it was identified for many years, but amphitheatres normally have two walls, one around the arena and another some distance from it to support the seating bank, and there is little trace of an outer wall here. Nor is there any reason why the substantial seating bank which would have existed should not have survived as a visible feature as it did at Caerleon. Alternative explanations are more difficult to find, but one which is favoured by some writers is that it was a cattle market

Even if Caerwent lacked a purpose-built amphitheatre, this does not mean that the people of Caerwent were denied their share of blood sports, for there was a long tradition in the Roman world of using the central court of the forum as a temporary arena.

The mansio

Immediately inside the south gate of the city, but probably long predating it, was a large residential building which has been identified as a *mansio*. These were inns placed at regular intervals on the major roads of the Empire to provide accommodation and fresh mounts for imperial messengers and others travelling on state business. Access to the *mansio* was very strictly controlled to prevent the system being abused. The costs of maintaining the building were probably borne by the Silures, although few members of the tribe would have been entitled to use it.

Religion

Most of the people living in Caerwent were Silures and, while they were willing to offer token allegiance to the Roman state deities, they had their own traditional gods. The Roman authorities had few objections to such religions provided that they did not threaten the state, and while they had done their best to extirpate the Druids, in part because they practised human sacrifice, the

63

The Romano-Celtic temple

Just to the east of the forum are the remains of a small Romano-Celtic temple and its associated buildings. Originally excavated in 1908, it was re-excavated in the 1980s when its plan and date were clarified. One surprise was the discovery that it had not been built until *c.*330, a time when Christianity was fast becoming the official religion of the Roman Empire, and its appearance in the centre of a tribal capital reminds us that we are near the edge of the Roman world where old customs lingered.

In plan the temple is a square within a square, the inner square being the main shrine (*cella*) which rose above the roof of the surrounding ambulatory. Its door faced the main entrance of the walled enclosure (*temenos*) around the temple, an area which would have been as sacred as the temple itself. Across the end of the *temenos*, against the street, was a long hall with an apsidal end and opposed doors in its longer walls. Clearly this hall was an important part of the religious complex, possibly used for religious ceremonies or as a secondary shrine. Later in the century a range of five rooms was added to the northern side of the apsidal hall, and, perhaps at the same time, a pair of statue niches built on either side of the door into the temple. Unfortunately we have no evidence of the deity to whom the temple was dedicated.

cults of Iron Age Britain continued almost unchanged throughout the Roman period (Chapter 10).

We cannot be certain if any of the temples in the city were the responsibility of the tribal council. They would have been expected to maintain the Roman state cults but these were probably housed in the basilica and did not require a separate building. The central position of the fourth-century temple which stood to the east of the forum suggests that it was of some importance, but we know nothing of its dedication although it would almost certainly have been to a native rather than a Roman deity. Such temples were usually supported by their own adherents.

Other temples existed within the city – one, a large octagonal building set in the centre of a circular enclosure, was found just outside the eastern wall of the city in 1912.

A good example of a private cult was a shrine discovered in the yard of a large house in Insula XI, just inside the west gate of the city. It took the form of a small, open-fronted structure with three steps leading up to a platform on which stood a large sandstone head. It dates from the fourth century AD and it confirms the evidence of the temple by the forum that a large part of the population of Caerwent remained loyal to their traditional deities well into the fourth century, despite the increasing Christianization of the Roman state (Chapter 10).

In fact there is only very slight evidence for Christianity in Roman Caerwent. A pewter bowl, one of several found together, has the *chi-rho* monogram (representing the first letters of the name of Christ in Greek) scratched onto it, although this need not mean that the rest of the set were used in Christian services. It has also been suggested that part of a house in the north-eastern corner of the town (House 22N in Insula V) had been adapted as a 'house church', a form of church not uncommon in the fourth century, although we have undisputed evidence for only one in Britain, in the villa at Lullingstone, Kent. But the identification of the Caerwent room as a church depends on its apsidal plan and is not easily accepted without some supporting evidence. No doubt Caerwent would have become increasingly Christianized throughout the fourth century, but, as elsewhere in Britain, the process has left little archaeological evidence.

Shops and workshops

It is not surprising to find that the majority of the buildings in Caerwent were either houses or shops and workshops. The excavators of Caerwent followed the practice of their day in only clearing the upper levels of the buildings which they found. The result is that their work provides us with the plans only of the many stone buildings which existed in the last years of Roman Caerwent. Only in a few cases have more recent excavations shown how such buildings had developed over time.

Economic realities applied as much in the Roman period as they do today, and it is not surprising to find that much of the main road in the centre of the city (Insulae VII, IX, XII and XIII) was lined with shops. Their street frontages were usually quite narrow, reflecting the high property values of such commercially desirable sites, but they extended back for some way, often with a small group of rooms at the back where the family lived. In some cases they may have had an upper floor. Only one group of such buildings can be seen today, at the junction of Pound Lane with the main road through the village which follows the line of the main street of the Roman city. This group was excavated in 1947–8 when archaeological techniques had become more refined, and as a result we know rather more of their development. The earliest structures on the site were a pottery kiln and a timber building, both dating from the later first century. The pots produced in the kiln include a type of flagon which is usually only found in military contexts in Britain, and which may hint at the existence of an early fort in the area. The first stone buildings were two typical workshops/shops constructed in the mid-second century. They have a long, relatively narrow front room, no doubt the shop, where some of the goods on sale were probably made. Behind it was the family's home consisting of two pairs of rooms set on either side of a passage running across the shorter axis of the building. Entry to this part of the building was through a door into the passage, not from the shop itself. A narrow alley ran between the two shops – a necessity in a period when gutters were unknown and rainwater ran straight off the roofs. Only the foundations of the walls remain, but it is likely that the stonework was no more than a footing for a timber-framed superstructure. There is no evidence for or against their having had an upper floor. The fact that there is a wall foundation at the front of the shops does not mean that they were cut off from the street; most probably they had wooden shutters which could be removed during the day. This was a common arrangement in the ancient world and one seen in many shops in Pompeii.

Early in the third century the workshop of the western building was damaged by fire, after which the domestic parts of the two buildings were joined together. The discovery in the western workshop (which was the only one to be completely excavated) of a possible forge with an adjacent water trough suggests that it was a smithy. The final change came in the mid-fourth century. The western workshop continued in use, although it was divided into two by a cross-wall, but the other one was demolished to create an open yard. The main change was in the living quarters which were rebuilt to form a more spacious range of rooms, two with mosaic pavements. Clearly the owners either had risen in the world or had sold the building to a more prosperous family. To the passer-by the most obvious sign of the changes would have been the construction of a portico along the street frontage. The house and its workshop continued to be occupied well into the fifth century when the Roman institutions of Britain were disintegrating, but it became more basic as time went on, with industrial hearths in former living rooms and pits cut through the mosaic floors. Life continued in Caerwent, but in this case at least, it was losing the refinements of the Roman world.

Houses

Most of the houses stood either behind the buildings which fronted the main east–west road or at its ends. Looking at the overall plan of the city one is struck by the fact that almost all the houses are relatively large, some having frontages extending for more than 30 metres (100 feet). No doubt such houses belonged to the tribal aristocracy, the men who served as decurions and dominated both the city and the tribal territory.

One of the basic building blocks of Roman architecture was a row of rooms fronted by a corridor or veranda. In its simplest form it is the military barrack block, or a small villa, while in the towns it appears as a simple house (as with Insula XVIII, Building 11s), or as one of several ranges of rooms surrounding a courtyard. There are several fine examples of this type of house in the city, including one immediately inside the West Gate (Insula XI, 7s), and Houses 2s and 3s in Insula XVI. Identifying the function of the rooms in such houses is not easy; the main one, often facing the entrance to the courtyard is likely to have been the dining room, but others are less easily identified. Some had mosaic floors, although few of those found at Caerwent were of high quality and almost all had geometrical motifs rather than figural scenes. Most of the houses seen on the plan are likely to be of fourth-century date, but only in two cases do we have details of how they had developed over time. One is a courtyard house behind the shops on the Pound Lane site, parts of which were excavated soon after the Second World War, and the other is slightly further to the north in Insula I.

The Pound Lane house was built in the first half of the fourth century on a previously unused area behind the workshops which we have already described. Thirteen rooms in two wings arranged around a large courtyard were excavated. Most were rather utilitarian with concrete floors, but one, in the north-west corner, had a mosaic floor and hypocaust heating. The house in Insula I, which was excavated in the 1980s, was more elaborate and had developed over a longer period of time. It was built on a plot of land which had remained open until the end of the second or early third century.

The first building, which was not fully excavated, had been demolished late in the third century and replaced with a new house consisting of two ranges of rooms set on either side of a central corridor decorated with a mosaic floor. This building was demolished in its turn and a much larger and more complex house, with ranges of rooms set around two courtyards, was built on the site early in the fourth century. Most of the rooms around the southern court were unpretentious in their decoration, and one, which had a raised floor, may have been a store for perishable goods, probably foodstuffs. However, the fact that at least one of these rooms contained a hypocaust while two others had plain tessellated floors suggests that they were the living quarters of people of some importance in the household. But the main domestic quarters were around the northern court, where many rooms had been decorated with painted wall plaster, and two had been heated with hypocausts and floored with simple mosaic pavements.

The fact that both of these houses were built on sites which remained open until late in the second century in the one case and until the fourth century in the other, suggests that large parts of Venta Silurum remained undeveloped for much of the history of the city, although it would be unwise to assume that this applied throughout the city. Recent excavations at Silchester in Hampshire, a city originally excavated at the same time as Caerwent, have shown that some of the areas where the early excavators had failed to find any buildings were actually filled with rather insubstantial structures, and the same probably applies at Caerwent.

The city defences
Today the most impressive features of Venta Silurum are the city walls, which are over a mile long and which enclose the ancient town and much of the modern village within an irregular rectangle. Most visitors are unaware that these walls, the finest of their type to survive in Britain, were a relatively late addition to the city. For the first century of its existence it lacked any form of defence, and when defences came they took the form of an earthen bank with a deep V-sectioned ditch in front of it. The walls themselves were not added until much later, and the impressive towers later still. There were four gates, one in each side. It is generally assumed that the original gatehouses were built of wood, probably looking very similar to those found in first-century forts, but the earthwork defences of some cities, most notably

The earthwork defences of Romano-British cities

The sequence of defences seen at Caerwent is typical of the cities of Roman Britain. Dating such defences is difficult, but the evidence suggests that most, though not all, the tribal capitals were given earthwork defences towards the end of the second century. Permission to defend cities, which might then be used as strong points in a civil war, was not granted lightly and was certainly not within the gift of the governor of the province. The fact that so many were defended at much the same time strongly suggests that these defences were a response to a specific threat, real or perceived. But what that threat was is less clear. Britain was involved in a civil war in the mid-190s and this has often been taken to be the reason for these earthwork defences. The argument is that the governor, Clodius Albinus, having made a bid for the imperial throne and knowing that he would have to take his army to the Continent for a final showdown, had the cities of Britain defended in case they were attacked by barbarians while the army was absent. Certainly the fact that they were defended with earthworks rather than stone walls is suggestive of haste, for such defences could be constructed in a fraction of the time it would have taken to build stone walls, but there are alternative explanations. The historians of the later second century rarely mention Britain, but there are enough references to suggest that there were recurrent problems throughout the last years of that century, and if we had more details these might offer equally good explanations for the defence of the cities.

Verulamium and Cirencester, are thought to have had masonry gatehouses which were later incorporated into the walls, and it is possible that this was the case at Caerwent.

The addition of stone walls to the earthwork defences of British cities was not a single event but was spread over many years, mainly in the third century, a fact which suggests that while they were regarded as necessary they were not built in response to a single emergency. One factor which must have controlled their construction was their enormous cost which would have been far greater than that of any building in the city.

The walls were inserted into the front of the bank, which was cut back to receive them, and in places they still stand to a height of over 5 metres (17 feet), and originally they probably rose to 7.5 metres (25 feet). At the base they are 3 metres (10 feet) thick, but this was reduced by a series of offsets in the back of the wall to about 2 metres (6 feet 6 inches) at the top where there was a wall walk fronted by battlements. At intervals the wall was continued at its full width to the top to create wider platforms which may have been intended to support steps up to the rampart walk or to carry artillery (*ballistae*). The core of the wall is formed of roughly cut stones set in mortar, but it is faced with carefully squared stones and where the facing has been robbed away one can see the straight joints which mark the junctions of lengths of wall built by different gangs of workmen.

The walls are usually dated to about 330 on the evidence of a coin found below one of the towers in material which is thought to have come from the construction of the wall itself. If so, they are exceptionally late, surprisingly so for a city close enough to the Bristol Channel to have made it an obvious target for barbarian raids. That such raids were thought to be a real threat is shown by the construction of the fort at Cardiff in the third century (Chapter 12).

There were four gates in the walls, of which the east and west ones on the main street were the most important, although the fact that the modern road still passes through them means that little of the gatehouses remain. What does survive shows that they had double portals flanked by large rectangular towers projecting in front of the walls. The north and south gatehouses were smaller with a single portal and probably with a tower above it. In the middle of the fourth century the walls were strengthened by the addition of large external polygonal towers on the north and south sides. Such towers were a feature of late Roman defences and allowed the defenders to fire along the face of the wall at attackers who had reached its base. Similar towers, significantly also polygonal in plan, already existed on the third-century fort at Cardiff and the decurions of Caerwent may have been familiar with those, although by the fourth century they were a standard feature of town defences on the Continent. Unfortunately the new towers projected over the line of the outer ditch and it had to be replaced with a new one 8 metres (26 feet) further out.

The further modification to the defences was the blocking of the portals of the north and south gatehouses and the demolition of

The gang-chain from the Iron Age votive deposit at Llyn Cerrig Bach, Anglesey, showing how it was used.

The foundation trenches of the timber granaries in the legionary fortress at Usk under excavation in 1969. Each granary was 120 Roman feet long and 40 Roman feet wide (116.5 × 39 feet or 35.5 × 11.8 metres) with its floor supported on 225 timber posts set in 25 trenches.

Legionary armour and equipment worn by a member of the Ermine Street Guard Roman Army Re-enactment Society.

Auxiliary armour and equipment worn by a member of the Ermine Street Guard Roman Army Re-enactment Society.

A copper alloy plaque from Caerleon showing a winged Victory carrying a trophy, consisting of a helmet and breastplate flanked by two shields mounted on a pole. It may be a fragment of parade armour as it is too elaborate to have been used in battle.

Ivory tragic mask from Caerleon, probably from a burial but originally mounted on wooden furniture.

Cornelian intaglio from a ring found in the main drain of the baths at Caerleon showing the goddess Roma, the personification of the City of Rome. Second century.

The reconstructed gate of the second-century fort at South Shields, at the mouth of the River Tyne, Tyne and Wear.

The walls and external towers at Caerwent.

Excavations in the basilica and forum at Caerwent in 1969.

their towers – a move clearly designed to strengthen the defences by reducing the number of weak points, for gates were the obvious places for an enemy to attack. The date of this work is unknown but it may have been done when the towers were added to the walls or soon after.

Carmarthen (Moridunum Demetarum)

We have little information on the Demetae who occupied Pembrokeshire and western Carmarthenshire. As we have seen (Chapter 4) very few forts are known in their territory, and while some may remain to be discovered, the area can never have been strongly garrisoned. Carmarthen itself was the site of a fort built in about 75 on the north side of a crossing of the River Tywi (to the east of the later castle) and closed soon after 120 when troops were needed to garrison Hadrian's Wall. Presumably the Roman authorities handed the site over to the Demetae for their new city, which was on the site of the *vicus* of the fort, when they were granted self-government.

Scarcely anything was known of the Roman town until the 1970s, since when a series of excavations has provided important, though tantalizingly incomplete, details of the development of the city. The major public buildings have not been excavated, but we know of a number of Roman domestic and commercial buildings, several apparently used by metalworkers. In the north-western corner of the town the earliest buildings were timber shops and workshops, which were rebuilt in stone in the third or early fourth century, only to be demolished later in the fourth century and replaced with a large house with a colonnade on the street front, a very similar sequence to that seen at Caerwent. Elsewhere the excavators have found a generally similar pattern with much use of timber as a building material. A typical Romano-British temple, similar to that found near the forum in Caerwent, has been excavated in the north-western quadrant of the town. Built late in the first century, it had been demolished before the end of the second century. The only public building known is the amphitheatre which lay over 200 metres to the east of the town walls, although, since it was built early in the second century, it predates them by some years and would originally have stood on the edge of the early town. When the town was defended it was probably not thought worth the expense of extending the defences to include the area around the amphitheatre. Only the arena wall and the entrance passages were built of stone; one of the outer retaining walls of the seating banks was cut into the hillside, the whole being constructed of timber.

The defences of the city follow much the same pattern of development as at Caerwent, with the construction of an earth bank fronted by two ditches in the mid to late second century. The area enclosed was 13 hectares (32 acres), which, even by Romano-British standards, made it a very small city. The date at which the wall was added remains uncertain, although it was probably in the mid to late third century. No external towers have been discovered, but since the wall is entirely levelled, this does not mean that none existed.

To anyone accustomed to the great cities found elsewhere in the Empire, Moridunum would have seemed very small and very provincial, but as a symbol of Roman success in persuading the peoples on the fringes of the Roman world to accept their customs and ideas it has more significance. In an area which was almost devoid of other aspects of Romanization, it was a beacon of civilization.

9 The Countryside

Most of the people of Roman Wales lived in the country and not in cities. We do not know what the population of Wales was at this time, but we can safely say that only a few thousand, certainly less than 10,000, lived in Caerwent and Carmarthen. No more can have lived in the various minor settlements and in the *vici* outside the handful of forts which were occupied after the 120s, although the fortresses at Caerleon and Chester had *canabae*, civilian settlements outside them, whose populations may have been numbered in the low thousands. Everyone else lived in the country, and most of them probably never even saw a city.

Vici

Most forts which existed for any length of time attracted civilians who catered for the needs of the soldiers. These people lived outside the fort in rather disorganized settlements known as *vici* (or *vicus* in the singular) which were smaller and poorer versions of the settlements (*canabae*) around the legionary fortresses. Most forts in Wales had such *vici* which disappeared when the forts were closed. The *vici* of the few forts which continued to be occupied after the middle of the second century were rarely occupied for as long as the fort itself, and this may reflect the fact that, as has been argued in Chapter 7, such forts had a largely administrative role and held a much reduced garrison which would not have generated a large *vicus*. There have been relatively few excavations on the *vici*, but where there have, at sites such as Caersŵs, Trawscoed and Brecon Gaer, they have revealed that most of the buildings were relatively small houses and workshops, although a substantial stone building at Brecon Gaer may have been a *mansio*, an inn used by men travelling on state business similar to the one at Caerwent (Chapter 8). In a few cases, where the economic conditions were right, these *vici* may have developed into small settlements after the closure of the fort, Usk and Abergavenny being two examples.

'Small towns'

Cities such as Caerwent and Carmarthen were not the only form of urban development in Roman Britain, and we know of a considerable number of largely unplanned settlements which never acquired a separate legal status and which were rarely defended. They probably developed in response to economic needs, particularly a demand for markets in areas which were some way from the tribal capitals, and it is not surprising that most lay on major roads. They are quite common in the more Romanized parts of England, and it is another reflection of the lack of Romanization in much of Wales that they did not develop at all in most parts of the country, and are relatively rare even in the southeast. Although the evidence is limited, such settlements existed at Abergavenny and Monmouth, both probably coming into existence after the closure of forts. Another example was at Usk where a large and sprawling settlement grew up on the site of the early fortress. Most settlements of this type were probably almost entirely dependent on agriculture, serving as a market and a source of tools and equipment, but at Usk and Monmouth ironworking was another important element in their economy.

The most extensive of these settlements was at Cowbridge, which is probably the 'Bovium' mentioned in the Antonine Itinerary, a list of routes and the places on them where travellers on state business could stay or get fresh mounts. Extensive excavations in parts of the modern town have revealed a small bathhouse as well as workshops and houses fronting the road to west Wales. The fact that the builders of the baths had used tiles with the Legio II Augusta stamp on them suggests that there was some official involvement in the settlement, as does the fact that the baths were closed early in the second century when the settlement was still in its infancy. However, the excavations have failed to find the fort which would be the obvious explanation of the presence of the bathhouse, although this does not mean that it did not exist. Several kilns for drying corn confirm that agriculture was an important part of the economy of the settlement.

Small settlements are known at Prestatyn, Pentre, near Flint, and Ffrith in north-east Wales which were probably connected with the lead industry of the region. At Pentre strip buildings and furnaces confirm an industrial function, while the existence of a large building, originally constructed of timber but rebuilt in stone in the mid-second century when stamped tiles of the Twentieth

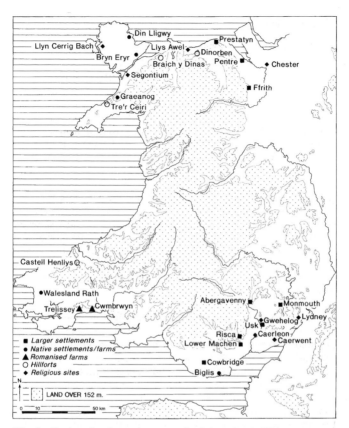

The distribution of native settlements and religious sites in Wales.

Legion at Chester were used, suggests that the settlement had an official element. Similar tiles have been found in a small bathhouse at Prestatyn, and at Ffrith, and it is possible that all three sites were used by the officials who oversaw the lead industry in the area, the officers of the *procurator metallorum*. Interestingly all three settlements either came to an end, or show signs of much reduced activity, after the mid-second century – possibly reflecting a decline of the local industry. Similar settlements probably existed in south Wales at Risca, where a bathhouse has been found, and Lower Machen. Both are relatively close to Caerleon, and both were probably associated with lead mines (Chapter 11).

Native settlements

At the time of the conquest there were several types of settlements in Wales. Hillforts were almost universal, but they were supplemented by settlements which were either undefended or enclosed by stone walls or banks and ditches which were too slight to be defensive. They vary in detail from one area to another, but in all cases the huts within them were circular, although they could be built of timber or have stone walls, largely depending on the local geology (Chapter 1).

The aim of the Roman government was to persuade the inhabitants of its new province to adopt Roman ways and customs, and this would have applied as much in the country as in the towns. Iron Age society was predominantly rural, and the social structure of the Iron Age continued into the early Roman period; indeed it probably continued in a slightly modified form right through it. This meant that the tribal leaders, the men with whom the Romans were primarily concerned, would have been more at home in the country than they were in new cities. The Roman government knew that, in a society as hierarchical as that of Britain, once the leaders had accepted the Roman way of life the rest of the people would either follow or at least accept Roman rule, even if Roman ways remained largely alien to them. In reality the Roman government had very little interest in the people living in remote rural areas and, provided that they caused no trouble – which they were unlikely to do without the encouragement of their tribal leaders – they were largely left alone to accept or ignore Roman ways.

The physical sign which is usually taken to indicate the acceptance of Roman ideas in the countryside is the appearance of the villa, a type of building which was quite different from the native round house. If this criterion is applied to Wales, we find that Romanization occurred only in a few areas in the south of the country. This is not surprising for the two cities of Wales, Caerwent and Carmarthen, are in this area as are most of the smaller Romanized settlements, such as Cowbridge. This situation was not unique to Wales; villas and towns are largely absent from most of northern England, especially the north-west, and the west Midlands. The older forms of settlement continued with only minimal changes throughout the Roman period in many parts of Wales. In the north-west, for example, where stone-founded huts in walled enclosures were common, we find that many of those that were first occupied in the Iron Age continued to be used well into the Roman period. Bryn Eryr on Anglesey, for example, which was founded as early as the third or fourth century BC, was still in use in the third century AD. Graeanog and Cefn Graeanog II, both in Caernarfonshire, began slightly later in the Iron Age but continued to be occupied until the fourth century AD. In all these the inhabitants lived in small groups of round huts, usually no more than two or three in number, in a way which was hardly affected by the Roman conquest. In these areas coins and even pottery were relatively rare, a significant fact when we remember that great quantities of pottery are found on most rural sites in the more Romanized parts of the province. It is this paucity of Roman artefacts as much as the continued use of Iron Age settlement types which shows how little north-west Wales took from the Roman world, and there can be little doubt that their social structure and religious ideas would have been equally unaffected by the coming of Rome.

We can only guess at the social status of the people who lived in these settlements. The evidence from those excavated suggests that primarily they were farms, and at first sight they might be thought too small and unimpressive to be the homes of the tribal nobility, but if they are not it is difficult to see where that nobility lived. A few sites are somewhat more impressive. Din Lligwy on Anglesey, with its cluster of stone huts of varying shapes and dates enclosed within a strong wall, is one, but it is only slightly larger and stronger than other sites in the area. Nonetheless we should remember that the buildings at Din Lligwy probably took as much time and effort to build as the average Roman villa, and more than one commentator has suggested that it was the social equivalent of a villa. The relatively rich artefactual assemblage from the site helps to confirm its higher status. It may be that the aristocracies of the tribes in Wales were generally less hierarchical than in some of those in England, with the result that there are fewer obvious distinctions of wealth.

These sites were in the north-west of the country far from the cities which were the centres of Romanization, but even in the south of Wales a similar situation existed in many places. In much of the south-west we find the same enclosures in use in the Roman period as in the late Iron Age. Walesland Rath, Pembrokeshire, which was first occupied in the third or second century BC, was not abandoned until the second century AD, by which time the inhabitants had become sufficiently Romanized to have built a rectangular hut to complement the round ones which were still in use. Even that degree of Romanization was relatively unusual, for the majority of huts retained a round plan throughout the period. Further east in Glamorgan we find a similar picture. Biglis, near Barry, began life as an open unenclosed group of huts at the end of the first century BC or the beginning of the first century AD, and after a break in occupation was reoccupied and enclosed within a palisade in the second half of the second century AD, the palisade being replaced by a bank and ditch in *c.*270. Throughout this period all the internal huts appear to have been round in plan; indeed it is only the pottery and other finds which show that we are not dealing with an Iron Age settlement. Biglis lay in the centre of the one part of Wales where the villa was widely accepted, and it would be interesting to know something of the social status of the family or families living there. Did they own the land, or were they the tenants of some greater landowner, perhaps living in one of the villas in the area? On the other hand, by concentrating on the types of buildings used on these sites we may be in danger of over-emphasizing the 'native' aspects of such settlements. The finds from the site show that the people of Biglis accepted many aspects of Roman life; what they rejected were the new house types which were only one aspect of Roman culture.

Nor were the old hillforts always abandoned. The Roman authorities did not necessarily discourage the continued use of hillforts, although the maintenance of their defences might have been another matter, but in many areas the convenience of living in less exposed places probably led to their abandonment. However, a number of Welsh hillforts have produced evidence of occupation in the Roman period. In a few cases the occupation may have continued through from the Iron Age: Braich y Dinas, Caernarfonshire, is probably the best example, and the well known site at Tre'r Ceiri in the Llŷn Peninsula may be another. Others seem to have been abandoned after the Roman conquest and then reoccupied. Dinorben near Abergele in Denbighshire, for example, was not reoccupied until late in the third century. In the south-west of Wales the small hillfort at Castell Henllys near Nevern was abandoned only for a new settlement to appear in an annexe adjacent to it. However, in some cases this late Roman activity may have been connected with a resurgence in the religious use of hillforts rather than resettlement, for a number of late Roman temple sites are known in English hillforts, Lydney being the most relevant to Wales (Chapter 10).

Romanization in the country

It was inevitable that those areas which were in contact with the newly developing Roman cities would begin to reflect Roman ways, for the native leaders who were being encouraged to adopt Roman customs are unlikely to have left them behind in cities when they returned to the country. The physical signs of this change can be observed in the types of building which begin to appear in rural areas, and the things which the people there used. Other changes, perhaps of greater significance, such as the use of Latin, are less easily detected. Latin never replaced the Celtic language for everyday purposes, but it was the language of official business, of the army and, most importantly, it was the written language; literacy and Latin were synonymous in Roman Britain. The surviving evidence suggests that the use of Latin was greatest in the cities and around the forts, and least in the depths of the countryside.

Archaeologically the key indicator of Romanization in rural areas is the appearance of the *villa*. A number of factors were required before a landowner and his family abandoned their traditional way of life and the buildings which were part of it. They had to become familiar with Roman buildings, and they had to accept that such buildings were not alien structures to be observed but not imitated, and this took time. Another factor was the need for the resources to fund new buildings. This probably did not arise with the early villas which were simple buildings, but the later, larger villas with their mosaic pavements and bathhouses required a substantial investment. Such wealth could come in various ways. There is no reason to doubt that the basic tribal structure survived throughout the Roman period and this would ensure that the aristocracy received an income, perhaps rent of some kind although not necessarily in the form of money. Another source of wealth was from the sale of surplus agricultural produce, although for this to be profitable there had to be a convenient market. In reality this meant a town, for the army, which might be

The villa

In Latin *villa* means no more than a farm, and that is what most of them were, but the Romans themselves used the word more loosely and in common parlance it came to mean almost any house in the country above the level of a peasant's cottage. In provinces such as Britain the term is usually limited to buildings which show several aspects of Romanization. The first of these was the adoption of that fundamental unit of Roman architecture, a series of rectangular rooms with a corridor in front. To this were added the use of masonry, of basic iron fittings such as hinges and nails, of plastered walls, often elaborately painted, of terracotta or stone roofing tiles, and of window glass. Later came the heated bathhouse and mosaic pavements. As a result, *villa* covers a multitude of building types ranging from simple farmhouses to vast palaces. But two factors are constant: the building is in the country, and it has the characteristics of a Roman building rather than a native one.

thought of as an alternative market, acquired most of its food through taxation in kind. Unfortunately, the geography of Wales, with its mountains and high moors, remote valleys and fast-flowing rivers, meant that in many areas a surplus was not easily produced, and where it was the cost of moving it to a suitable market was often prohibitive. The exceptions were the coastal areas of south-east Wales where, as we have seen, two towns did come into existence.

The relationship of the city and its countryside was a complex one, and the factors which led to the development of viable towns were much the same as those needed for the Romanization of the countryside. In south Wales there were large areas of good land, while the new military roads made the movement of goods relatively easy, if rather expensive. Fortunately the Severn estuary and Bristol Channel allowed bulky goods to be moved more easily and gave access to markets on the other side of the Bristol Channel (Chapter 11). Fragments of a late third-century boat found near Magor to the east of Newport provide unusually concrete evidence for such traffic. The result of this combination of circumstances was the development of both towns and villas. Once the process

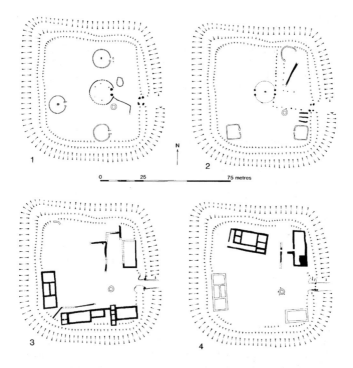

Plans of the Iron Age farm and Roman villa at Whitton. 1. At the time of the Roman conquest AD 55–75, showing the earthwork defences and four timber huts. 2. AD 115–35, showing the rectangular huts and a small granary to the south of the gate. 3. AD 230–80, showing the stone buildings. 4. AD 300–40, showing the new stone buildings.

was under way other factors began to play their part, for Roman Britain was the recipient of all of the technical knowledge of the Roman world. Equally important was the widespread acceptance of a monetary economy, a major contribution to the mechanism of exchange. Individually these factors meant little; together they were critical. Where they did not apply, as was the case with much of Wales, the old ways continued largely, although not completely unchanged.

81

Villas

When compared with some parts of England the villas of south Wales are both few in number and, in most cases, distinctly basic. Almost all lie in the area between the Wye and the Tywi estuary, with the majority in and to the east of the Vale of Glamorgan, while another series runs south from Wroxeter through the Marches, mainly on the English side of the border. Most were and remained simple farms; only a few, notably Llantwit Major, developed sufficient wealth for us to regard them as country houses whose owners may not have been totally dependent on the surrounding land for their income. Very large and imposing villas comparable with Woodchester in Gloucestershire or Bignor in Sussex are completely lacking.

As a result of recent excavations we now know that most villas originated as farmsteads in the late Iron Age, and that they were probably the homes of the tribal leaders and their more important

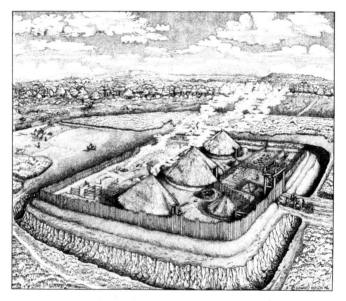

Reconstruction of the Iron Age farmstead at Whitton in AD 55–75. (Drawn by Howard Mason)

followers. In Wales this is seen most clearly in the small villa at Whitton near Barry. The fact that the site was relatively compact meant that it could be completely excavated, and Michael Jarrett elucidated the full complexity of its development in a series of excavations in the late 1960s. The buildings lay within an enclosure some 60 metres (200 feet) square, surrounded by a bank, *c.*4 metres (13 feet) wide and originally *c.*2 metres (6.5 feet) high, outside which was a ditch averaging 5 metres (16.5 feet) wide and 2 metres (6.5 feet) deep. These 'defences' are too slight to have presented a serious obstacle to a raiding party, and, like so many enclosures in Iron Age Britain, they were probably designed to protect the inhabitants and their animals from thieves and to stop animals from straying. There was a single entrance with a small tower above it, a feature intended as much to impress visitors as to strengthen the defences. Inside the enclosure were three round timber huts, of typical Iron Age type, each about 10 metres (33 feet) in diameter. This first phase probably began sometime after AD 30, perhaps twenty years before the Romans arrived in the area. Surprisingly little changed for the next eighty years. The huts were rebuilt and, although the defences were allowed to decay, the gatehouse was maintained, presumably for reasons of prestige. This continuity of Iron Age customs well into the Roman period is not abnormal; they offered no threat to the Romans who were quite happy to leave them alone.

The first sign that the inhabitants were open to Roman ideas came early in the second century when they built two new wooden huts using the same techniques as before but square in plan. There can be little doubt that this rectangularity reflected Roman buildings, and this inference is strengthened by the fact that they also built a small rectangular granary, its raised floor supported on posts set in three parallel trenches, a miniature version of the granaries seen in Roman forts of this date. It was another twenty years before the first stone-founded building appeared on the southern side of the enclosure, a simple rectangular structure which may have had timber-framed walls. At the same time two new timber granaries were built to replace the original one. And so the slow sequence of change continued. In the middle years of the second century other stone-founded buildings were erected, and a room heated by a hypocaust added to the original building. The third century saw further changes. By now the farmstead had become thoroughly Romanized, but the buildings were functional, relatively comfortable no doubt, but hardly luxurious. Although the defences had long since been levelled, the farm must still have

Reconstruction of the Roman villa at Whitton in AD 300–40. (Drawn by Howard Mason)

been enclosed, perhaps by a palisade or hedge, for the gates were regularly replaced. By then the south range had been extended for almost the whole length of the enclosure, but it was a series of rooms rather than a unified building. One oddity of this period was the construction of two sets of rooms apparently intended for hypocausts although these were never actually built. One of them, a group of four tiny rooms, must have been designed as a miniature bath-suite, similar to one excavated in the equally small villa at Llandough, between Penarth and Cardiff. At about this time a new house, consisting of four rooms, was built on the west side of the enclosure, with the result that the central yard was now almost entirely surrounded by buildings.

The steady process of change continued into the fourth century, a time when many villas in England reached the apogee of their development and wealth. The changes at Whitton, however, were less spectacular, although a new house was built on the north side of the enclosure with a large central room, groups of smaller

The villa economy

In their essentials villas were farms, probably producing a mixture of animals and cereals. At Whitton the latter are vouched for by the succession of simple granaries which were later replaced by one of the barns, while fragments of palisades in the yard suggest the need to control stock. The animal bones from the site indicated that cattle and sheep were present in equal numbers, although when it is remembered that, in terms of edible meat, a single cow is the equivalent of several sheep it is clear that beef was the favoured meat. The fact that sheep also produced wool and that both cows and sheep could be milked doubtless added to their value. Pigs were less common than cattle and sheep by a factor of three to two, but their presence suggests that there was woodland, their traditional habitat, near the villa. The only other farm animals found were horses, which may have been eaten as well as used for riding and traction, and dogs, mostly of terrier types. There were enough deer bones to show that hunting was popular, but the weight of meat produced was too little to have made venison a common dish; red deer outnumbered roe deer by about two to one.

rooms at its ends and a corridor at the front. The foundations were unusually deep, which may indicate that, unlike the earlier buildings, it had an upper floor. Whether the older buildings on the south and east sides of the enclosure were still in use at this time is uncertain, but the excavators thought that they could have been, although possibly serving a more utilitarian function. The site was abandoned by about 340, although there were no signs of violent destruction to suggest that it was destroyed in a barbarian attack.

It seems very likely that this slow development over several centuries was typical of the villas of south Wales. Romanized they were, but it took many years for the process to be completed, and their owners never had the desire, or resources, to acquire the trappings of luxury. The Llandough villa was very similar to Whitton, although there the owners completed their bijou bath-house.

Villas such as Whitton were probably the norm in much of the Vale of Glamorgan and in the areas further west. There are a

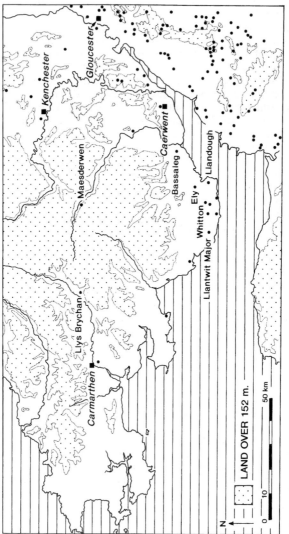

The distribution of villas in south Wales and parts of Gloucestershire and Somerset.

LAND OVER 152 m.

50 km

Kenchester
Gloucester
Caerwent
Maesderwen
Bassaleg
Llandough
Ely
Whitton
Llantwit Major
Llys Brychan
Carmarthen

N

0   10

number of small, Romanized farms, rather like the early stone phases of Whitton, in Carmarthenshire and Pembrokeshire. The best known are at Trelissey (Pembrokeshire) and Cwmbrwyn (Carmarthenshire), and both are set within enclosures as at Whitton. Unfortunately, they were excavated many years ago and the history of their development is not known. They mark the edges of Romanization, as does a rather more elaborate villa with hypocausts which was partially excavated at Llys Brychan, north of Carmarthen in the Tywi valley. All of these probably reflect the influence of Carmarthen which must have acted as a centre of Romanization in this rather remote area.

To the east of the Vale of Glamorgan a number of probable villas are known in Monmouthshire, including a small cluster near Caerwent, and another recently discovered by aerial photography near Bassaleg, on the edge of Newport. Much further north at Maesderwen in Breconshire, far removed from any of the obvious centres of Romanization, a large bathhouse with fine mosaics of fourth-century type was excavated in the eighteenth century. Its position and apparent wealth make it a complete anomaly.

Few of these possible villas have been excavated, and many were probably relatively simple buildings comparable to Cwmbrwyn, but two villas in Glamorgan were rather more elaborate, although the history of their development is less well understood. The first at Ely, on the outskirts of Cardiff, was excavated in the late nineteenth and early twentieth centuries. If there had been a timber phase – and it is probable that there was – the early excavators did not detect it. What they found were two separate buildings lying more or less at right angles to one another and linked by a wall. The northern building was a typical small villa, consisting of a central block with short projecting wings at its ends and a corridor running between them. At the back was a pair of long, narrow rooms. In its basic plan it is not dissimilar to the houses built at Whitton in the fourth century, and it is probably of similar date. The second building was a long block, divided into three rooms, to which a small bathhouse was soon added. At the beginning of the fourth century this second block was demolished and the northern building surrounded by a roughly rectangular enclosure. Occupation ended at some time in the second quarter of the fourth century. Although agriculture must have formed the basis of its economy, ironworking debris suggests that this was an additional source of income.

The most elaborate villa to have been excavated in Wales was at Llantwit Major, further west in the Vale of Glamorgan. This was a

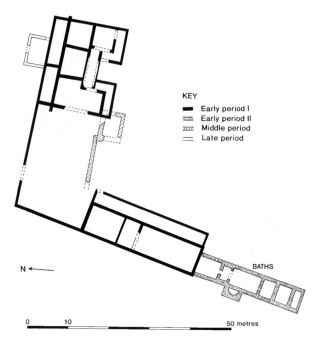

KEY
▬ Early period I
▨ Early period II
▨ Middle period
═ Late period

N ←——

BATHS

0   10   50 metres

Plan of the villa at Ely.

far larger and grander affair than Whitton or Ely. The main house consisted of a large L-shaped block which defined the northern and western sides of a yard, with another block on its southern side and two separate but linked buildings, both probably barns, to the east. The main living rooms of the villa were in the northern wing of the main house, one having a mosaic floor. The southern end of the west wing included a small bathhouse. The southern building was a 'basilican' house, a type which had a nave flanked by aisles, the north aisle here being divided into four rooms with two more at its west end. Such buildings are sometimes associated with other forms of villa buildings, as here, or they may be the only building on a site. At Llantwit Major it may have provided quarters for the farm workers, or it may have been a store building, or both. A geophysical survey of the site has revealed that there is at least one other large building which has never been excavated.

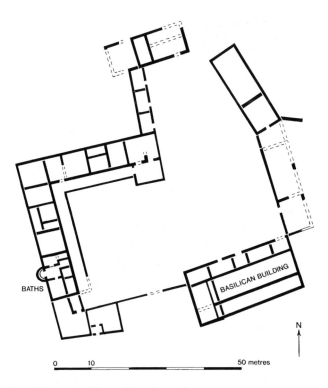

Plan of the main buildings of the villa at Llantwit Major.

V. E. Nash-Williams, the excavator, believed that the whole complex was constructed in one phase, but comparison with other villas whose histories have been more fully elucidated suggests that this is unlikely. A small excavation in 1971 in the room with the mosaic pavement confirmed that the final phase of the house was preceded by a long and complex development. The plan suggests that the main house was formed by linking up a series of separate blocks, of which the north wing was originally a free-standing winged house similar to that at Ely. Its history may have begun in the late Iron Age, and the existing stone phases were probably preceded by a series of timber buildings, for which the excavations did produce some slight evidence. Occupation of the villa continued well into the late fourth century, but when and how it ended is uncertain. The discovery by the nineteenth-century excavators of the skeletons of humans and horses within the building led to a suggestion that it had ended in a massacre, but burials found in more recent excavations were quite normal, and it seems that the area was used as a burial ground after the villa itself had disappeared.

10 The Religions of Roman Wales

The Roman world had many religions and the imperial government tolerated most of them. The result was an exceedingly complex mixture which, while varying from one part of the Empire to another, almost always had certain basic elements: the Roman state religion; the Classical Graeco-Roman pantheon; the 'mystery religions'; and the native gods of the region. The Romans themselves were accustomed to a pantheon of deities and they found it easy to accept the gods of other peoples. They might object to some aspects of particular cults, but only rarely to the cult itself. Thus the practice of human sacrifice which was common to all the Celtic peoples was unacceptable to the Romans and they did their best to extirpate it, but they appear to have made no attempt to suppress the worship of the gods involved.

Roman state religion

It is hardly surprising that the imperial government expected the peoples of its Empire to accept the deities who presided over the fate of Rome and its Empire. In Roman theology there was a clear relationship between man and the gods, and it was largely one of agreements; if men did not fulfil their share of the bargain it put the whole relationship in jeopardy. The Roman gods had granted the city and her people unparalleled success, and in return the Roman world was required to worship them. This might involve no more than dropping a pinch of incense on the altar but it had to be done. Since the Romans were polytheists they felt people who were unwilling to acknowledge their gods must be motivated by a desire to break the bargain between Rome and its gods with all that that would entail, and at that point Roman toleration ended, as the early Christians discovered when they refused to make such sacrifices.

The three gods worshipped on the Capitol in Rome – Jupiter, Juno his consort and Minerva – personified Roman state religion. Together they formed the Capitoline triad, and most Roman cities had a temple or shrine dedicated to them – a *capitolium*. In many Continental cities this took the form of a large temple in the forum complex, but this was not normally the case with British cities, although Verulamium in Hertfordshire was an exception. In Britain the triad was probably worshipped in a shrine in the basilica together with the second strand of the state religion, the imperial cult. This was the worship of emperors, and some of their consorts, who had been deified by the Roman Senate, alongside which there developed a cult of the ruling emperor and his family. Their worship was of particular importance for the Roman army, where loyalty to the imperial family was paramount if revolts were to be avoided.

The majority of people in Roman Britain were probably perfectly happy to accept this arrangement. They too were polytheists and had no problem in accepting the Roman deities, but in most cases their worship would have been a formality which did not extend into their private lives.

Roman deities

The gods of the Roman pantheon were not widely worshipped in Wales, and most of the references to them are found in inscriptions from Caerleon and other military sites where soldiers from the Continent brought their gods with them. It is at Caerleon that we find inscriptions referring to such Classical deities as Jupiter, Diana or Nemesis. Another inscription comes from Segontium (Caernarfon) where a soldier dedicated an altar to the goddess Minerva. More are known from the fortress of the Twentieth Legion at Chester where there are dedications to Jupiter, Mars and Minerva, as well as to the gods of medicine and health (Aesculapius and Salus), and, rather ominously, an altar to Nemesis in the amphitheatre. Salus alone appears on an altar from Caerleon. Although most of the native Britons probably had little interest in the Roman gods, they were well aware of their existence for, as we shall see, they often conflated them with their own deities in inscriptions.

Mystery religions

The Roman gods offered their worshippers little prospect of a meaningful afterlife, a spiritual gap which for many was satisfied by various cults originating in the Eastern Empire and beyond. These are the mystery religions, so called because many aspects of the cult and its ceremonies were mysteries revealed only to the initiates. Most were selective in who they admitted and new members usually underwent some form of initiation ceremony. Their appeal lay in offering the initiate a personal relationship with the god and, if the initiate obeyed the rules, which usually inculcated a moral life, they promised a desirable afterlife. We have evidence for a number of these cults in Britain but only two, Mithraism and Christianity, can be proved to have reached Wales. The cult of Mithras originated in Persia but by the time it reached Britain it had become thoroughly Romanized. Membership was limited and women were excluded. It appealed especially to merchants and army officers, and the evidence for it in Wales is from military sites. An inscription from

The Caernarfon Mithraeum

Mithraea are known from a number of military sites in Britain, mainly on Hadrian's Wall. In common with other 'private' temples they were built outside the forts, and one can be seen at Carrawburgh in Northumberland. *Mithraea* have many features in common; they were windowless with an entrance porch (the *narthex*) which opened onto a nave with long benches on either side where the worshippers reclined at the sacred banquet which was an important element of the ceremony. At the far end was a relief or painting showing Mithras slaying the bull, a scene which symbolized the triumph of good over evil, in front of which stood various altars. In the army the cult appealed particularly to the officers and it was they who built and maintained the *mithraea*.

The Segontium *mithraeum* was excavated by George Boon in 1959 and, although it was not well preserved, it was possible to show that it had had the usual plan with a recess at its end for the relief of Mithras slaying the bull – although the relief did not survive. Four altars were found but only one bore an inscription, the initials of the man who dedicated it; the others may have had painted inscriptions. The *mithraeum* was probably built in the second half of the second century, continuing in use until late in the fourth century when it may have been destroyed, as were so many *mithraea*, by Christian zealots.

Caerleon refers to 'The Invincible Mithras', and we may assume that somewhere outside the fortress there was a temple to the god, but the best evidence is the small *mithraeum* found outside the fort of Segontium, modern Caernarfon.

Christianity, with its offer of salvation for its followers, was similar to the other cults, although it differed in various ways, most obviously in its monotheism. This was one of the causes of its regular clashes with the Roman state for, as we have seen, a refusal to make a token offering to the Roman state religion was regarded as incipient treason by the Romans. For Christians, however, such an offering would be a betrayal of their faith, and some preferred martyrdom to political expediency. The two martyrs, Julius and Aaron, who probably died at Caerleon in the mid-third century have already been mentioned (Chapter 5). The other evidence for Christianity is more conventional: a pewter bowl from Caerwent with the chi-rho monogram scratched on it. The suggested house church at Caerwent cannot be regarded as proven (Chapter 8).

Native deities

The great majority of the people of Roman Wales, both in town and country, probably continued to worship the gods of their ancestors. Unfortunately, in most cases they did so without leaving any archaeological evidence for their beliefs. Although some of these native gods appear to have been worshipped over a wide area, in some cases covering large parts of Gaul and Germany as well as Britain, others were more localized. The subject of 'Celtic' religion is complex, but in essence it was concerned with the forces of nature, with the need to propitiate deities who were not inherently benevolent towards mankind, in order to ensure the regularity of the seasons and the fertility of crops and animals. Unlike the Roman gods, who usually confined their interests to one or two aspects of human life, many of the native deities were less restricted in their concerns, although the geographical areas over which they exercised their powers might be limited. Indeed, in some cases they appear to have been very restricted and have been centred on a spring or some other natural feature. The best known of these is the goddess Coventina whose spring lay just outside the fort at Carrawburgh on Hadrian's Wall, but the popularity of holy wells in the Christian period suggests that she may have had relatives in Wales. A Roman version of this is seen in the altar erected near Chester by the Twentieth Legion to

'The Nymphs and Fountains', a reference to the springs which supplied the fortress with water.

In many inscriptions the names of the native deities are equated with those of Classical gods, as with Mars Ocelus on an altar from Caerwent. Syncretism of this type occurs throughout the Roman world; we see it, for example, in the association of the Syrian god Dolichenus with Jupiter on an inscription from Caerleon.

One of the most important elements in the worship of these deities was sacrifice, for offerings were needed to placate hostile deities and to gain the goodwill of others. If a request was made to a god it had to be accompanied by an acceptable offering, although this might be withheld until the favour had been received. Hence the use of the formula *VSLM* on the Mars Ocelus dedication. The favoured offering was usually a blood sacrifice; in the Roman period it was an animal, probably a cow or sheep in most cases, since the sacrifice of human beings was forbidden by the Roman authorities. At intervals throughout the Iron Age, particularly at the beginning and at the end, we find large hoards of metalwork either buried or thrown into bogs or rivers, the best known being that from Llyn Cerrig Bach on Anglesey (Chapter 1). There is little doubt that most of these hoards were ritual offerings, although we do not know to whom they were offered. Similar votive hoards, often placed in pits or wells and dating from the Roman period, are known in England, but at present we have no such deposit from Wales.

Many of these native deities probably had no temple of their own, but others did, and we find such temples in both the towns and the countryside, although the number known within Wales is extremely limited. The Celtic temple at Caerwent has already been discussed in Chapter 8, and another is known from Carmarthen. The only example of a rural temple in Wales has been discovered by aerial photography at Gwehelog near Usk. It is circular in plan and stands in its own enclosure (*temenos*) together with some ancillary buildings. We know from examples in England that many Roman rural temples were built on the sites of earlier Iron Age wooden temples. In most cases it was the excavation of the masonry temple which led to the discovery of its Iron Age predecessor, and if, as seems probable, they continued to be built of timber in many parts of Wales throughout the Roman period, they are unlikely to be discovered.

Pilgrims visiting such temples, particularly those in the country, often offered small bronze statuettes of the deity or of animals

Mars Ocelus

The written language of Roman Britain was Latin and there are many Romano-British inscriptions referring to native deities. However, the act of putting their names into a Latin inscription often encouraged the worshippers to equate them with the Roman deity who was closest to them in function, or to that aspect of their often multifaceted nature which the worshipper wished to emphasize. An interesting example is a small altar from Caerwent dedicated to the native god Ocelus who was equated with Mars, the Roman god of war. The inscription reads:

DEO MARTI / OCELO /AEL(IUS) AUGUSTINUS OP(TIO) /VSLM

To the God Mars Ocelus, Aelius Augustinus, optio, willingly and deservedly fulfilled his vow.

An *optio* was the deputy, or adjutant, of a centurion who took charge of the century in the centurion's absence, and it provides evidence of the close links which must have existed between Caerwent and the legion at Caerleon. Both Roman and native religions involved agreements made between human beings and their gods, and if the deity fulfilled his or her part of the agreement the human suppliant had to reciprocate. *VSLM* (*votum soluit libens merito*) is the formula which indicates that Mars Ocelus had granted Aelius Augustinus' plea and that by erecting the altar Augustinus was completing his part of the agreement.

associated with it. The site at Lydney, which is discussed below, has produced a number of statuettes of this type, including one of the finest and most realistic portrayals of a dog known from Roman Britain. A small group of statuettes of Mercury and three dogs found at Llys Awel, Abergele, can only be a votive deposit, and they suggest the presence of a temple in the area. The dog was often associated with healing cults in the Romano-Celtic world.

One of the finest of all rural sanctuaries is at Lydney in the Forest of Dean just outside the boundaries of modern Wales. For many years it was thought to have been built in the second half of the fourth century, but recent excavations and fresh studies of the

The altar to Mars Ocelus from Caerwent.

coins from the site have shown that it was actually constructed in the second half of the previous century. It lies within the ramparts of an Iron Age hillfort overlooking the Severn estuary. Most rural sanctuaries consisted of the *temenos*, or sacred area, within which stood a temple usually similar to that at Caerwent, but Lydney was more complex. The god venerated there was Nodens who was identified with Mars, although at Lydney he was worshipped as a healing god – an example of the diverse nature of many native deities. The temple, which can still be seen, had a central *cella* or

The Lydney dog. A bronze statuette showing a wolfhound from the Roman temple at Lydney, Gloucestershire. Dogs appear to have been sacred to the god Nodens who was worshipped at Lydney.

shrine with side aisles which continued behind the three open-fronted 'chapels' at the end of the *cella*. In its original form the worshippers could pass from the *cella* into the aisles. Each of the outer walls had two recesses reminiscent of the side chapels of some medieval churches. After some years part of the temple collapsed and in the subsequent restoration the *cella* was separated from the aisles, and the recessed chapels walled off to form small rooms. At the same time a mosaic with a dedicatory inscription was laid in the shrine, the gift of a man whose title on the inscription was abbreviated to *pr rel*. Unfortunately this may be expanded in various ways. For many years it was argued that it referred to the officer in charge of a supply depot of the fleet, and cited as evidence for such an establishment on the Severn at Lydney, but more recently it has been suggested that it simply meant 'superintendent of the cult', a man who may have interpreted the dreams of the worshippers, a reference to the unusual nature of the cult. Fortunately, all agree that the mosaic was dedicated to Mars Nodens.

The other buildings of the complex were more unusual for such a sanctuary. They include a large building with a central courtyard which has been identified as an inn for visitors to the sanctuary. A large room facing the entrance may have been a communal dining room or a reception hall. By its side, on the edge of the steep scarp of the hill, was a bathhouse. The third building, which stood behind the temple, consisted of a long row of rooms fronted by a corridor or veranda. Mortimer Wheeler, who believed that the complex was a healing sanctuary where the sick went to be healed by Nodens, suggested that this building was a dormitory in which pilgrims slept in the hope that the god would appear to them in their dreams and either heal them, or tell them what to do in order to recover. Such dormitories are known in healing sanctuaries in the eastern Mediterranean, but whether this is the explanation of the building at Lydney is less certain.

11 Trade and Industry

Crafts

The distinction between crafts and industries was not clearly defined in the ancient world, and most of the things used in daily life were either made in the home or produced by craftsmen working in the community. The discovery of large numbers of spindle whorls on both urban and rural sites show that spinning was a common occupation in the home, while the discovery of the weights used in simple looms confirms that weaving was also done in the home, particularly in rural areas. Other craftsmen to be found in the cities and settlements, and probably in the larger villas as well, who are known from both their products and their tools, include masons, smiths, carpenters and leather workers. There is evidence of metalworking from many sites, both in the towns and the countryside. The smithy in Pound Lane in Caerwent has already been mentioned (Chapter 8), but small hearths used either by blacksmiths or for melting copper and bronze are common discoveries. Less common was the series of furnaces, probably used to convert iron to steel, that were found at the late Roman settlement at Usk.

Imports

Other products were brought into Wales. Until late in the second century the finest tableware was the glossy red samian ware produced in Gaul and imported into Britain in vast quantities. By the mid-second century potteries in England were producing acceptable tablewares and the discovery of such pots throughout Wales confirms that there was a network of traders to distribute them and, doubtless, other goods which do not survive in the archaeological record. But most of the pots used in the kitchens in the cities and for almost all purposes by the peasants were often produced locally, although the *mortaria* used for grinding and mixing foodstuffs continued to be brought from a few major centres in England. Glass was another product which was imported in large amounts. Although there is evidence for glass-making in England the finest glass was imported, mainly from the Rhineland, although pieces from Italy and further afield are known from early sites such as Usk. Glass, including window glass, was common in the cities and villas, but a rarity in the more remote country areas.

There is little doubt that a trade in perishable materials, particularly in food and drink, also existed, but we can only detect it when the containers used to transport the products have survived. Wine and olive oil are the most obvious, and both must have been regarded as necessities by the legionaries of the first and early second centuries who came from the Mediterranean world. Fragments of oil and wine amphorae are found in large numbers in the fortresses at Usk and Caerleon and in the early forts. Later, as the proportion of soldiers from the Mediterranean provinces declined, so did the demand for these goods, but a certain amount continued to be imported throughout the Roman period.

Industries

Although the bulk of goods were produced close to where they were used there are a number of exceptions, including stone-quarrying, the production of pottery and tiles, and the smelting of metals. Obviously the first is dependent on the location of the stone, while the others required furnaces or kilns which were a major fire risk in urban areas as well as producing noxious fumes and smoke. Once the ore was smelted the metal was often worked in the cities, for the furnaces and hearths which were required were relatively small and operated at lower temperatures than the smelting furnaces.

Quarrying and stone

Quarrying must have been an important industry in south Wales where mortared stone was widely used. A little stone, such as the fine Italian marble found at Caerleon, was imported but such stones were only used where prestige was more important than cost and such buildings were rare in Wales. Most stone was quarried locally, but there is good evidence that some stones were moved considerable distances. One example is slate from the Prescelly Mountain in Pembrokeshire which was found in the wharves at Caerleon. It may have come to the fortress as ballast, but it proves that cargo ships were sailing around the coasts of

Wales, and that slate was being quarried in Pembrokeshire, an area not otherwise obviously integrated into the industrial economy of Roman Wales. Bath stone was also quite widely used in south Wales, especially for architectural detail, although a local sandstone from Sudbrook had to suffice for the Corinthian capitals of the columns in the basilica at Caerwent, and this stone was also used at Caerleon.

The army played its own part in the quarrying industry. Almost all the forts which survived into the second century were at least partially rebuilt in stone quarried locally, probably by the soldiers themselves. The army had begun to work some quarries soon after it arrived in Wales, for local stones were used in the foundations of the streets and for the bath building in the fortress at Usk, and a nearby source of gritstone was used to make honestones on an almost industrial scale. Both soldiers and civilians needed large numbers of quernstones to grind flour. Mills, driven by animals or waterpower, did exist but they were relatively rare, although a fragment of a millstone was found in the villa at Whitton (Chapter 9). Most people, including soldiers, particularly when they were in the field, ground the grain with a pair of quernstones. Such stones are common finds on Roman sites and in Wales they are usually made of local stones. The main exceptions are from military sites, because the army in the first century imported many quernstones from Germany made from a form of lava which produced exceptionally efficient querns. Some of these are found on civilian sites, including Whitton, but most of the querns used by the natives were made of local sandstone. The army was equally quick in exploiting outcrops of stones which were suitable for making quernstones. Even within the lifetime of the fortress at Usk, which was closed before 75, outcrops of sandstone some 8 kilometres (5 miles) away were being used to make querns, while at the other end of Wales most of the quernstones from the fort at Segontium (Caernarfon) were made of local stones.

The pottery industry

At the time of the Roman conquest pottery was almost unknown in many parts of Wales. The result was that the army, which used immense quantities of pots, had to organize its own supplies, which it did by importing pots from other parts of Britain and Gaul, and by setting up its own kilns which were usually attached to the legionary fortresses. Although the kilns at Usk have not been found, there is no doubt that the Twentieth Legion had its own pottery outside the fortress, probably, but not certainly, staffed by members of the legion. Most of the pots produced there were derived from types found in the Rhineland and Upper Danube regions, no doubt the areas where the legionary potters had learned their trade before they were moved to Britain. In the second century pottery was being made locally for the Second Legion at Caerleon, although the fact that the potters were illiterate suggests that they were not actually legionaries. A large industry would have been required to make the vast number of bricks and tiles needed when the fortress was being rebuilt in the second century. Many of the tiles are stamped LEG II AVG, probably in a not wholly successful attempt to prevent their misappropriation. Auxiliary forts did not normally have their own kilns, but there were some exceptions in Wales, probably because the forts were far from the centres of production, and isolated

The legionary kilns at Holt

The kilns which supplied the fortress at Chester were at Holt on the River Dee, 12 kilometres (7.5 miles) from the fortress. As it is almost certain that they lay within the land annexed to the legionary fortress they provide an indicator of the great extent of a legionary *territorium*. The kilns were part of a complex of buildings which included barracks for the workers, probably mainly soldiers, a house for the commandant in charge of the establishment, and a bath building. As well as the kilns there were two workshops where the pots and tiles were made and dried before firing. Most Romano-British kilns are relatively small, circular structures, but the kilns at Holt were a different affair. The main group contained six large rectangular kilns built of tiles encased in a sandstone jacket; half of them had been used to fire pots, and two for tiles of varying types, many stamped with the name of the Twentieth Legion. Most of the pottery produced was for general use, but some fine green-glazed pottery was also made. The complex was probably built at the end of the first century, when the rebuilding in stone of the fortress at Chester began, and continued in use until the middle of the third century. Its situation on the River Dee was no accident, for it allowed the products to be carried to the fortress by water.

kilns have been found or postulated at Loughor, Gelligaer, Caersŵs, Trawscoed and near Tomen-y-mur and probably Caernarfon, some making tiles as well as pottery.

We know less of the civilian pottery industry in Wales. The economic need to have relatively large markets fairly close at hand meant that there were large parts of Wales where very little pottery was produced. More than one pottery existed near Cardiff, but the only site to have produced enough kilns to be called an industry was at Caldicot in Monmouthshire, which would have had a ready market for its products in Caerwent.

Mining

Wales is a land rich in minerals, and both metals and coal were exploited in the Roman period. In most cases we have little knowledge of the mines themselves for they have usually been destroyed by later workings, but other evidence shows that the industry was widespread in Wales. The metals sought were iron, copper, lead, silver and gold.

We know of no Roman coal mines but the coal itself has been found at various Roman sites in south Wales. None dates from before the late second century which suggests that the industry took some time to become established. Recent analytical work has shown that both Usk and Caerleon received coal from the Pontypool/Risca field, no doubt brought along the Usk valley, and that some coal from that field also reached Caerwent, which obtained additional supplies from the Avon and Somerset field on the English side of the Bristol Channel. Another coalfield was that in the Forest of Dean, and it is not surprising to find coal from there at Monmouth, although its discovery in the villa at Llantwit Major is more unexpected. However, the villa is quite close to the Bristol Channel, which suggests that the coal was being shipped to customers in the Vale of Glamorgan.

Under Roman law the state held all mining rights and usually leased the mines to contractors, although at times the army might be involved. Whether iron mines were strictly controlled is uncertain; most of our evidence is concerned with more valuable metals, and iron ore is so common that the state may have done no more than tax the major workings. Two late Iron Age sites in Snowdonia (Crawcwellt and Bryn y Castell) have produced evidence of large-scale iron smelting in an area which would not normally be associated with iron mining, and this utilization of

104

local resources continued into the Roman period when there was a resumption of production at Bryn y Castell in the second century. However, the main centre for iron mining in western Britain was the Forest of Dean. Most of the orefield lies in England, but there is enough evidence from Monmouth and other sites around it to show that the production area extended into Wales. The only certain Roman iron mines are at Lydney where small, tortuous tunnels burrowed into the hilltop. Lydney is on the fringes of the main ore field and mines elsewhere may have been larger and more sophisticated. There are important deposits of iron ore in Glamorgan, and while most of the alleged 'Roman' mines found by later miners are likely to be Tudor or even later in date, analysis of Roman slags found in Cardiff Castle suggests that they were derived from ores mined at Lesser Garth to the north of the city.

Lead ores usually contain a proportion of silver and they were mined by the Romans for both metals. Some of the Welsh ores had quite a high silver content and Welsh silver may have been an important element in the economy of north-east Wales. However, analysis has shown that some of the lead mined in Britain contained so little silver that Roman metallurgists were unable to extract it, in which case it must have been the lead alone which was sought. As we have seen, a number of settlements in north-east Wales seem to have been centres of lead production (Chapter 9). The Romans needed huge quantities of lead, primarily for plumbing, but also for such things as weights, coffins, water tanks and to make pewter, an alloy of lead and tin which was widely used for tableware in later Roman Britain. The lead would have been smelted near the mines and the raw metal taken out in the form of ingots (pigs), weighing 80 kilograms (176 pounds) or more, which often bear cast inscriptions. From these we know that lead was being mined on the Mendips by 49, just six years after the invasion, under the supervision of the Second Legion. Some ten years later entrepreneurs had leased some of the Mendip mines, and the name of one, C. Nipius Ascanius, a freedman who was probably funded by a wealthy Roman backer, also appears on a pig from Carmel in Flintshire, indicating that he had obtained a mining lease in Flintshire. Unfortunately the pig is undated, but others from Chester date to 74. These, and some others, bear the word *Deceangl(i)*, the name of the tribe mentioned by Tacitus who occupied modern Flintshire. We have less evidence from the south of the country. A fragment of a pig from Caerwent with a Second Legion stamp confirms a military interest in the metal, although it does not mean that it was mined locally. Roman lead mines are known at Draethen near Machen (Gwent), although what is known of these does not suggest a very high level of investment.

A considerable number of bun-shaped copper ingots have been found at various sites in north Wales and these confirm that the copper ores of the area were exploited at that time, but we have little information on the mines themselves. Two ingots from Parys Mountain bear the stamp of a lessee named Julius, while another from Aberffraw, also on Anglesey, bears the stamp of the *Sociorum Romae* (the partners resident in Rome), another group of lessees. The discovery at Dinorben of a large stone mould for casting the bronze discs which were the first stage in the production of metal vessels shows that the copper was worked as well as mined in north Wales.

The most remarkable Roman mining complex in Britain is at Dolaucothi (Pumsaint) in Carmarthenshire, the only place in Britain where the Romans are known to have mined gold. It is a complex site, and, as so often with mining sites, the early workings have been confused and largely destroyed by later work, but what survives indicates a large and well organized enterprise. The mines lay near a fort but this may be no more than coincidence, although the military presence may have offered some security when they were first established. The most impressive surface feature is the aqueduct system which is over eleven kilometres (6.8 miles) long and which was capable of bringing some 13.6 million litres (*c.* 3 million gallons) of water to the mine each day. When it reached the mining area it flowed into a series of large tanks. Its function has been debated: one theory is that the water was pooled up and then released to scour the superficial deposits from the hillside and reveal where the lodes outcropped. But it seems unnecessary to have dug such a long aqueduct for such a limited purpose; indeed the men involved could probably have cleared the hillside in less time than it took to build the aqueduct. More recently it has been suggested that the water powered a series of heavy trip hammers which crushed the ore, but this suggestion presupposes that such hammers were known to the Romans, and this is still debated. Another use might have been to wash the crushed ore and separate the particles of metal from the fragments of rock. Most of the underground workings have been destroyed by later mines but a fragment of a large wooden waterwheel found in one of them shows that the Romans were using the most advanced mining technology to drain them. Treadmills of this type were worked by slaves or convicts, and a series of them would have lifted the water to the surface. The mine was probably worked by lessees, but no details are known. A hoard of fine jewellery dating to the late first century AD, including snake bracelets, was found in the area early in the nineteenth century. However, it was not made from the local gold, and its quality and value suggest that it could have belonged to the wife of the commander of one of the forts in west Wales.

12 The Later History of Roman Wales

No Roman historian after Tacitus specifically mentions Wales, a failure which forces us to rely on archaeology and the occasional inscription to produce a rather generalized account of the later history of Roman Wales. We have already seen (Chapter 4) that most of the forts in Wales were closed in the second century, although the legionary fortresses at Caerleon and Chester remained. This is the period which saw the increasing Romanization of parts of Wales, in particular the south coast. Over the rest of the country it appears that Rome and her customs were accepted without producing major changes in the lifestyle of the natives.

The first signs of the troubles to come appeared in the closing years of the second century. The assassination of the emperor Commodus on 1 January 193 began a civil war in which the governor of Britain, Clodius Albinus, made a bid for the imperial throne. A short truce with his main rival, Septimius Severus, ended in his death in a battle near Lyon in Gaul in 197. It was probably soon after this victory that Severus reduced the power of the governors of Britain by dividing the province and its military garrison into two, *Britannia Superior* and *Britannia Inferior*. Wales was in *Britannia Superior* with London as its capital.

We know from Roman historians that there was trouble in Britain both before Commodus' death and after Severus' accession, but they provide few details. A large part of Albinus' army must have come from Britain, but the idea that the removal of these troops was followed by a massive attack by the Scottish tribes on the north of England and as far south as Wales is generally discounted today. It is clear, though, that there were military problems in the north of England throughout Severus' reign, and that these were of sufficient gravity to justify his mounting an imperial expedition against the Scots. This began in 208, when Severus and his family came to Britain, and continued until his death at York in 211. His successor, Caracalla, was assassinated in 217 but his maternal relations managed to keep the succession within their own family until 235, when the murder of Severus Alexander initiated a period of instability in which emperor succeeded emperor, each devoting their time and the Empire's money to futile efforts to buy the loyalty of the army while the Empire was attacked by barbarians from all sides. Not until the accession of Claudius Gothicus in 268 did stability begin to return and the Empire recover its lost provinces.

What effect this had on Britain, let alone Wales, we do not know. The few historians of this period do not mention Britain, but the archaeological evidence does not suggest any major disasters. Yet, the fact that many towns had their earthwork defences strengthened with costly stone walls at this time suggests that a need for additional security was felt throughout the provinces of Britain. If, however, the dating evidence for the walls of Caerwent is accepted, it was not one of the cities defended at this time – perhaps because towns in Wales were not thought to be under as much threat as those of southern England.

The army in Wales in the third century

What we know of the military history of Wales in the third century does not suggest an imminent crisis. Inscriptions from Caerleon and Chester show that the fortresses were maintained and repaired under Severus and his immediate successors; an inscription from Caerleon records the rebuilding of barrack blocks as late as 255–60. At Chester recent excavations have shown that there was a major building programme early in the third century which completed several important buildings which had been left unfinished in the previous century. Inscriptions are rare in the auxiliary forts of Wales, but one records the restoration of an aqueduct at Segontium (Caernarfon) at the beginning of the third century. Cardiff, Castell Collen, Caersŵs and Forden Gaer in the Severn valley are the only other forts which appear to have been occupied at this time, although there may have been a small force at Brecon Gaer where a bathhouse was built within the fort. In all cases, save for Cardiff, these forts were probably serving as much as administrative centres as garrisons.

In 284 Diocletian, a man of formidable abilities, became emperor and, in collaboration with his colleague Maximian, undertook a complete reformation of the institutions of the Roman world in an attempt to make them better fitted for the problems and customs of the late third century. In Britain that process was delayed when, in 287, the commander of the Channel fleet, Carausius, seized control of Britain and northern Gaul. But his small empire was short-lived, and in 296 Constantius Chlorus, Constantine the Great's father, crossed the channel to destroy the army of Allectus, Carausius' assassin and successor, and to reunite Britain with the Empire.

One of Diocletian's reforms was to subdivide most of the existing provinces, with the result that Britain was divided into four provinces, Wales, together with the west of England, becoming *Britannia Prima* with Cirencester as its capital. Another major reform was the remodelling of the Roman army. By the end of the third century the constant crises on the Empire's extensive frontiers had led to the creation of a number of field armies with most of the auxiliaries and even the legions being reduced to little more than frontier guards. It was these changes which led Diocletian to reduce the strength of a legion from some 5,500 men to around 1,000.

The Forts of the Saxon Shore

The fact that Britain was an island saved it from the worst ravages of the barbarian invasions in the mid-third century which devastated parts of Gaul, but its long coastline left it open to attack from across the North Sea. To counter such attacks a chain of forts was built along the English coast from the Wash to Portsmouth Harbour, the whole system being known as the Forts of the Saxon Shore. These forts were designed to protect the coast against raids from the sea and they must have worked in conjunction with a fleet. We now know that the system was not designed as a single entity but developed over a period of somewhat over a century. The construction of these forts – together with the walling of the major towns – leaves little doubt that the Roman authorities felt that Britain faced a real threat, albeit one which in the absence of historical accounts we do not fully understand.

The changes of the third century must have affected Wales as they did every other part of the Roman world, but the archaeological evidence is ambiguous. The most obvious innovation was the construction of a large fort at Cardiff in the mid-third century.

Its towering walls with their external towers, lavishly restored in the nineteenth and early twentieth centuries by the marquess of Bute, give a good impression of the scale of the original defences. The walls enclose 3.6 hectares (8.8 acres), but excavations have failed to detect any substantial buildings within it; presumably its garrison lived in wooden hutments.

Cardiff and Lancaster are the only places on the western coasts of Britain where forts similar to those of the Saxon Shore were built. Cardiff was designed to guard the Severn estuary and must have worked in concert with a fleet, but whether it was primarily concerned with the defence of south Wales is another matter, for the Severn provided a route by which hostile ships could penetrate western England and raid the rich villas around Cirencester and those would have provided far better loot than any in south Wales. Whether Cardiff stood on its own is uncertain. There is some evidence to suggest that the forts at Loughor and possibly Neath may have been reoccupied in the later third century. If so, they must have liaised with the larger fort at Cardiff. The threats to which the Cardiff fort was a response can only be guessed at, but since a ship from northern Continental Europe would face a long voyage before reaching south Wales, it seems more likely that the raiders originated in Ireland. It seems clear that Ireland was the source of danger which led to the maritime defences found in north Wales.

It has been suggested that the new fort at Cardiff was a replacement for the legionary fortress at Caerleon where excavations have shown that several major buildings ceased to function at the end of the third century; the headquarters building, the hospital, the fortress baths and the amphitheatre were all either abandoned or demolished at that time. These changes are usually interpreted as indicating that the fortress was closed and the legion removed at that time, but there are a few other buildings, including some of the barracks, which were still in use in the fourth century. In any interpretation of this evidence we must remember that the Diocletianic reduction of the legion to about one-fifth of its original size will have resulted in fundamental changes in its physical requirements. The large buildings designed for the original legion would have been of little use to its far smaller successor, which may indeed have lacked the capacity to maintain them. Future excavations will probably solve this problem, but at the moment we cannot be sure if the much reduced legion did or did not remain at Caerleon in the fourth century. What we do know is that by the end of that century it was in garrison at the Saxon Shore fort at Richborough, Kent, where it is recorded in the *Notitia Dignitatum*, a late Roman list of public and military officials compiled at the turn of the fourth and fifth centuries.

The defences of north-western Wales

The only other defences built in Wales at this time are in the far north-west of the country, at Caernarfon and Holyhead, and were clearly designed against raiders from across the Irish Sea. The key site is Caergybi, an enclosure standing on the inner harbour at Holyhead. Although there is no independent evidence for its date, its design, with high walls and almost circular external towers, and the fact that it probably opened onto the harbour are strikingly similar to some fortified landing places built on the Rhine in the late Roman period. Rising above the town is Holyhead Mountain on which a small rectangular tower commanding wide views across the Irish Sea was built in the fourth century to act as an observation post for the base at Caergybi. Another site often linked with these is the enclosure known as Hen Waliau (Old Walls) just above the river at Caernarfon, to the west of the fort of Segontium. Unfortunately, its function and precise date within the Roman period are not clear and it may or may not have a naval connection. The lack of external towers argues against a late Roman date, but is not conclusive.

Segontium (Caernarfon) is one of the very few forts in Wales which was occupied until almost the end of the Roman period. The coins needed to pay the garrison continued to reach the fort until 393 when the supply was interrupted by a civil war on the Continent – never to resume, suggesting that the garrison was withdrawn at that time. The continuing Roman interest in this rather remote part of Britain is difficult to explain. It may have been the need to prevent enemy forces, in this case the Irish, from establishing themselves on the mainland, but it may also have been to protect the copper mines of Anglesey, if they were still active as late as this.

There are enough historical references to Britain to make it clear that there were a number of major crises during the fourth century. The most serious was in 367 when an alliance of tribes from Scotland, Ireland and the Continent made a concerted attack on Britain. While it is unlikely that the barbarians were capable of storming the walled cities, they did great damage in the countryside, and a field army had to be brought to Britain before the Romans were able to regain control. The involvement of the Irish in this attack confirms that the forts at Cardiff, Holyhead and Lancaster were a response to a real threat. Archaeologists have long observed that many villas, including some of those in south Wales, were abandoned in the middle years of the fourth century, and, while we are more hesitant today in ascribing this to the barbarian conspiracy of 367, we cannot doubt that it caused a great deal of damage.

The fourth century saw other changes in Roman Britain, particularly in the cities. It has been suggested that large parts of British cities were virtually deserted in the late fourth century, although there is sufficient evidence from others to show that this was not always the case. The early excavators of Caerwent were incapable of dating the buildings which they found, but the recent excavations have shown that at least some of the houses there were still in use in the late fourth century and probably later still. But Caerwent was not exempt from the changes seen in other British cities, the most dramatic change being in the basilica, which was used for industrial activities between $c.340$ and 370–80 when it was demolished (Chapter 8).

The man who defeated the barbarian invaders of 367 was Count Theodosius who appears to have successfully restored order in the province and undertaken a thorough overhaul of its defences. But nothing he did could prevent the inevitable decline of Roman power in western Europe, a decline which was accelerated by the repeated rebellions of ambitious generals. Britain had already seen two of these, Clodius Albinus at the end of the second century and Carausius at the end of the third. Now in 383 there came another, Magnus Maximus; a Spaniard by birth, he held a high military position in Britain and was popular with the provincial army. Like his predecessors his ambitions were not confined to Britain and he soon moved to the Continent, although he returned in 384 to fight a campaign against the Picts and Scots. By the late fourth century the Roman Empire had split into two, with the Eastern Empire being ruled from Constantinople and the West nominally from Rome, although the division was often blurred by the intervention of one emperor in the affairs of the other. Maximus' war was with Gratian, the Western emperor, who was unpopular with much of his army. The troops showed their dislike by deserting his cause and leaving him to be captured and killed, a victory which gave

A silver coin of Magnus Maximus.

Maximus control of Gaul and Spain as well as Britain. Theodosius I, who ruled the Eastern Empire, was willing to acknowledge him as the legitimate ruler of those provinces, but not of Italy. So when Maximus invaded Italy in 387, it inevitably brought him into conflict with Theodosius (a far more formidable figure than the unfortunate Gratian), who defeated Maximus in 388 and restored the unity of the Western Empire.

We do not know how many of the troops who fought for Maximus came from Britain, but it is difficult to believe that his imperial ambitions had had no effect on the British garrison. It used to be thought that he completely denuded Hadrian's Wall of men, but this idea is now disproved, as is the suggestion that he strengthened the defences of north Wales by moving Cunedda, a leader of the Votadini of south-eastern Scotland, and his followers into the area – a move which is now thought to date from after the end of Roman Britain. Nonetheless, for reasons which it is difficult to explain, Magnus Maximus made a deep and lasting impression on the people of Wales for he appears in the Mabinogion as Macsen Wledig, a great hero from whom many of the rulers of early medieval Wales traced their descent.

Maximus' revolt must have increased the doubts which the more Romanized part of the population probably had of the central government's ability to protect them, and justly so, for the end of Roman rule was fast approaching. Our main sources for this final period are the eulogies which the poet Claudian wrote for Stilicho, the Vandal general who effectively controlled the Western Empire between 395 and 408, and the writings of the sixth-century British monk Gildas – both of whom were experts in obscurity – together with a few references in later Byzantine histories. It appears that in 398 Stilicho sent troops to Britain to deal with invasions by the Irish, Picts and Saxons, an action which was completely successful according to Claudian. If so, it was a short-lived success, for in 401 Stilicho withdrew troops for more critical wars on the Continent.

The evidence which we have suggests that the last troops in Wales were removed in the final years of the fourth century. None of the Welsh forts are mentioned in the *Notitia Dignitatum* which was compiled at about that time. No new coins reached Segontium after about 393 and the *Notitia* lists a unit called the 'Seguntienses', who must have come from there, serving in the Balkans. The fortresses at Chester and Caerleon are absent from the *Notitia*, and the Second Legion, formerly at Caerleon and now, of course, a relatively small unit, appears as the garrison of the Saxon Shore fort at Richborough, Kent, the chief military port of late Roman Britain. All of this suggests that many of the troops in Britain were removed in the final years of the fourth century for service on the Continent, where barbarian invasions threatened the very fabric of the Roman world, but whether this was the result of a single decision or the actions of successive rulers remains uncertain.

The Roman government, faced with a series of disasters on the Continent, may have wanted to keep Britain within the Empire, but reality forced them to give its military requirements a low priority. Irish sources refer to attacks on the south coast of Britain by the High King, Niall of the Nine Hostages, probably in 405, and while England may have offered the richest pickings, it is unlikely that Wales emerged unscathed from such raids. Under these conditions it is not surprising to find what remained of the army in the island supporting a series of British usurpers. The first, Marcus, was hailed in 406 and killed in 407, to be succeeded by Gratian who ruled for four months. His successor, who bore the auspicious name of Constantine, had to face the fact that Gaul itself was slipping from Roman control and that, without Gaul, Britain could not survive as a part of the Roman Empire. In an attempt to save a rapidly collapsing situation he took his army to

Gaul in 407, only, after some initial successes, to fall victim to a revolt within his own territories and an attack by Honorius, the Western emperor, in 411.

Constantine's decision to take most of the remaining British garrison to Gaul must have been a blow to the civilians of Britain who, as Constantine's new empire began to crumble, found themselves owing loyalty to a ruler who was incapable of helping them against increasing barbarian attacks. The result was described by the late fifth-century historian Zosimus, apparently referring to events in 408–9: 'So the Britons took up arms and facing dangers for their own safety they freed their cities from the barbarians who threatened them.' But this example of self-help did not entirely destroy their hope of aid from the central authorities, for in 410, Zosimus records the response to an appeal to the emperor Honorius: 'Honorius sent letters to the British cities, telling them to look after their own defences.' It is interesting that this appeal was made to Honorius rather than to Constantine, who was not finally defeated by Honorius until 411; clearly the British cities had written him off as a possible source of help. The wording of the imperial response does not imply that Britain had been abandoned but that for the time being the emperor could not provide help. But hard reality was stated by the great Byzantine historian Procopius, who, referring to events in 411, wrote: 'Constantine was defeated in battle and died with his sons. Nonetheless, the Romans were no longer able to recover Britain, which from that time continued to be ruled by those who seized power.'

Further Reading

There are relatively few books concerned solely with Roman Wales, but most of the general books on Roman Britain have sections on Wales. Most of the general books listed here have long and detailed bibliographies referring to more specialized works and papers published in journals, such as *Archaeologia Cambrensis* and *Britannia*, which are the most important journals devoted to Welsh archaeology and Romano-British studies respectively.

Christopher J. Arnold and Jeffrey L. Davies, *Roman and Early Medieval Wales*, Stroud: Sutton Publishing, 2000.

Anthony R. Birley, *The* Fasti *of Roman Britain*, Oxford: Clarendon Press, 1981.

Kevin Blockley, *Prestatyn 1984–5: An Iron Age Farmstead and Romano-British Industrial Settlement in North Wales*, Oxford: British Archaeological Reports (British Series) no. 210, 1989.

George C. Boon, *Isca: The Roman Legionary Fortress at Caerleon, Mon.*, Cardiff: National Museum of Wales, 1972.

George C. Boon (ed.), *Monographs and Collections. 1 Roman Sites*, Cardiff: Cambrian Archaeological Association, 1978.

George C. Boon, *The Legionary Fortress of Caerleon-Isca*, Cardiff: National Museum of Wales, 1987.

Richard J. Brewer, *Corpus Signorum Imperii Romani. Great Britain Vol I, Fasc. 5, Wales*, London/Oxford: British Academy/Oxford University Press, 1986.

Richard J. Brewer, *Caerleon-Isca*, Cardiff: National Museum of Wales, 1987.

Richard J. Brewer, *Caerwent Roman Town*, Cardiff: Cadw/Welsh Historic Monuments, 1993.

Richard J. Brewer, *Caerleon and the Roman Army*, Cardiff: National Museum and Galleries of Wales, 2000.

Barry Burnham and Jeffrey L. Davies (eds.), *Conquest, Co-existence and Change: Recent Work in Roman Wales*, Lampeter: *Trivium* 25, 1991.

P. John Casey (ed.), *The End of Roman Britain*, Oxford: Oxford University Press, 1979.

P. John Casey, *Carausius and Allectus: The British Usurpers*, London: Batsford, 1994.

P. John Casey and Jeffrey L. Davies, *Excavations at Segontium*

(Caernarfon) Roman Fort, 1975–1979, London: Council for British Archaeology, 1993.

Simon Esmonde Cleary, *The Ending of Roman Britain*, London: Batsford, 1989.

Barry Cunliffe, *Iron Age Communities in Britain*, London: Routledge, 1991.

Cyril Fox, *A Find of the Early Iron Age from Llyn Cerrig Bach, Anglesey*, Cardiff: National Museum of Wales, 1946.

Sheppard Frere, *Britannia: A History of Roman Britain*, London: The Folio Society (3rd edition revised), 1999.

Willoughby Gardner and Hubert Savory, *Dinorben: A Hillfort Occupied in Early Iron Age and Roman Times*, Cardiff: National Museum of Wales, 1964.

Miranda Green, *Exploring the World of the Druids*, London: Thames & Hudson, 1997.

Miranda J. Green (ed.), *The Celtic World*, London: Routledge, 1995.

Miranda Green and Ray Howell, *A Pocket Guide: Celtic Wales*, Cardiff: University of Wales Press/ The Western Mail, 2000.

Stephen J. Greep (ed.), *Roman Towns: The Wheeler Inheritance. A Review of 50 Years' Research*, London: Council for British Archaeology, 1993.

Michael G. Jarrett, *Early Roman Campaigns in Wales. The Seventh Annual Caerleon Lecture*, Cardiff: National Museum of Wales, 1994.

Michael G. Jarrett and Stuart Wrathmell, *Whitton: An Iron Age and Roman Farmstead in South Glamorgan*, Cardiff: University of Wales Press, 1981.

Gwyn Jones and Thomas Jones (trans.), *The Mabinogion*, London: J. Dent, 1976.

Michael Jones, *The End of Roman Britain*, Ithaca, NY: Cornell University Press, 1998.

Jeremy K. Knight, *Caerleon Roman Fortress*, Cardiff: Cadw/Welsh Historic Monuments, 1994.

Frances Lynch, *Prehistoric Anglesey* (revised 2nd edition), Llangefni: The Anglesey Antiquarian Society, 1991.

Frances Lynch, Stephen Aldhouse-Green and Jeffrey L. Davies, *Prehistoric Wales*, Stroud: Sutton Publishing, 2000.

John Manley, S. Grenter and F. Gale, *The Archaeology of Clwyd*, Mold: Clwyd County Council, 1991.

William H. Manning, *Report on the Excavations at Usk 1965–1976: The Fortress Excavations 1968–1971*, Cardiff: University of Wales Press, 1981.

William H. Manning, *Report on the Excavations at Usk 1965–1976: The Fortress Excavations 1972–1974*, Cardiff: University of Wales Press, 1989.

William H. Manning, *The Early Roman Campaigns in the South-West of Britain. The First Annual Caerleon Lecture*, Cardiff: National Museum of Wales, 1988.

V. E. Nash-Williams (2nd edition, M. G. Jarrett (ed.)), *The Roman Frontier in Wales*, Cardiff: University of Wales Press, 1969.

Tim Potter and Catherine Johns, *Roman Britain*, London: British Museum Press, 1992.

David Robinson (ed.), *Biglis, Caldicot and Llandough. Three Late Iron Age and Romano-British Sites in South-East Wales. Excavations 1977–79*, Oxford: British Archaeological Reports (British Series) no. 188, 1988.

Peter Salway, *Roman Britain*, Oxford: Oxford University Press, 1985.

Peter Salway, *The Oxford Illustrated History of Roman Britain*, Oxford: Oxford University Press, 1993.

Charles Thomas, *Christianity in Roman Britain to AD 500*, London: Batsford, 1993.

John Wacher, *The Towns of Roman Britain*, London: Routledge, 1995.

Peter V. Webster, 'The Roman period', in H. N. Savory (ed.), *Glamorgan County History Vol. II. Early Glamorgan*, Cardiff: Glamorgan County History, 1984, pp. 277–313.

J. David Zienkiewicz, *The Legionary Fortress Baths at Caerleon*, Cardiff: National Museum of Wales, 1986.

Index